Crans-Montana
Switzerland

Farrol Kahn

Farrol Kahn
Farrol Kahn is the author of several
books including Riga and its beaches
(Landmark Visitors Guide), Oxford
(Landmark Visitors Guide) and Arrive
in Better Shape (HarperPaperbacks).
He lives in the Valais, Switzerland.

Published and printed by
Gutenberg Press Ltd
Gudja Road,
Tarxien Malta GXQ 2902

ISBN 978-3-9524208-0-5

Design and layout: AZZZA Limited, UK

Photo Credits: John Cosford

Acknowledgements

The author would like to thank the many people in Crans-Montana whom he met and helped him during the course of writing the book. In particular, Dave Albrecht, Isabelle Bagnoud-Loretan, Christian Barras, Gaston Barras, Liz Bestenheider, Carine Bestenheider, Géraldine Bestenheider, Jean-Claude Biver, Joseph Bonvin, Patricia Bonvin, Andrew Bushnell, Claudio Casanova, Christophe Chammartin, Dr Christian Schroeder, Francis Clivaz, Marielle Clivaz-Ketteridge, Ludivine Comina, Dr Christian and Béatrice 'Poupy' de Courten Sandra Crettenand, David and Elizabeth Duc, Catherine Antille Emery, Jean-Pierre Emery, Nati Felli, Georges and Kathleen Grintakis, Neva Hay, Rahel Isenschmied, Alexandar "Aco" Kalajdzic, Jeremy Kett, Yves Klingler, Sami Lamaa, François Lamaa, Claude-Gérard Lamon, Marc Lindner, Professor Pierre Magistretti, Erwin Mathieu, Tania Mathieu, Laurent and Marie-Anne Morard, David and Virginie Pasquiet, Julien de Preux, Steve Rey, Fabrice Rey, François Rielle, Philippe Ruboud, Daniel Salzmann, Muriel Schindler, Philippe Studer, Nicolas Taillens, Sylvie Taillens, Reto Taillens, Sonia Tatar, Eddy and Marlène van der Vliet and Lara Vocat.

A special thanks is given to Professor Pierre Ducrey, who assisted me so ably me with the intricacies of golf and its history and Richard Clifton with his translations.

Photo Credits: There were numerous sources for the photographs including my own. John Cosford who has now assisted me with two books, has earned a photo of himself and looks very James Joycean in the Ave de la Gare, Montana. Other credits include: Al Lopez (Marielle Clivaz-Ketteridge), Crans-Montana Classics ©Valais/Wallis Promotion, Crans-Montana Tourism, Crans-Sur-Sierre Golf Club, Gabriel SA, Guarda Golf, Hublot, International Summer, Camp Montana, Ferdinand Hodler - Les Étangs longs bei Montana 1915 SIK-ISEA Zurich, Nicolas Bagnoud, Isabelle Bagnoud-Loretan, Christian Barras, Eric Besse, Carine Bestenheider, Alexandre Borgeat, Michele Casamonti, Claudio Casanova, Francis Clivaz, Marielle Clivaz-Ketteridge, Ludivine Comina, Pierre Crépaud, Patrick Cretton, (SMC), Caroline Dechamby, Hervé Deprez, Catherine Antille Emery, Sandrine Espej, Rahel Isenschmied, Chris Masterson, Christian Perret, Franck Reynard, Daniele Salzmann, Phillip Zhan.

Contents

Introduction

What makes Crans-Montana so unique is not only its panorama, its year-round sunshine, the fantastic run from the glacier on Plaine Morte all the way down a 6,000-foot vertical drop to the village but its spectacularly scenic golf courses where the ball travels much further because of the high altitude. But insiders know there is more to Crans-Montana than just the high plateau. It comprises medieval villages and families like the Barras and Bonvin that go back to the 13th and 14th century respectively. There is also the tradition of vertical living through seasonal migration from the vineyards near the Rhone to the Alpine meadows and in-between.

But above all it is about the people as Crans-Montana is known for its openness to accept all comers. The categories include inhabitants of the mountain villages who are proud of their origins and traditions, the foreigners who have settled there and the apartment owners. Brief glimpses of people are given below which are expanded on later.

Francis Clivaz is a visionary from Bluche, a son of a postman, who together with his four brothers established a private school which taught subjects in English. Later, it was transformed into Les Roches, a top international school of hotel management with 2,250 students.

Erwin Mathieu is another success story who came from a poor village, Agarn, in the German part of the Valais. An anglophile, he once worked for Foyles bookshop in London and admired Christina Foyles' 1965 Rolls Royce Silver Cloud III. Now he has the same model in his car pool in Crans-Montana.

Doris Mudry who lives up in the Alpine meadows from June to September carrying on the ancient tradition of cheesemaking. She is up at 2 am every morning producing cheese from the previous day's milk.

Dr Christian de Courten whose family was ennobled by French King Louis XV because his ancestors were successful commanders and provided soldiers to fight in the king's army.

Gaston Barras has done more than anyone else to put Crans-Montana on the map. He is a latterday Renaissance man and in the United Kingdom would have been given a knighthood and titled Sir Gaston, but here has the sobriquet of Mr Golf.

François Rielle who lives in the resort cut his teeth in the property boom and became successful by applying Benjamin Franklin's aphorism about patience unknowingly in his business. Rielle believes that you must wait and to have the power to wait. Then the years will work for you and better conditions will prevail in the future.

Hervé Deprez is the third generation to run a photography shop in Montana. His grandfather was a Belgian soldier who came after World War I to recuperate after having been gassed. He stayed, studied photography in Vevey and married a local girl.

The 11 year old Pierre Magistretti and his brother who came from Milan were sent to school in Crans-Montana when their parents separated. The experience transformed him because he learnt to cope in unknown situations. He became a top golfer with a handicap of 1 and the youngest professor to occupy a chair at a Swiss medical school.

Liz Bestenheider who grew up in Los Angeles met her Swiss husband, Thierry, in the US. They returned to Crans-Montana to raise a family. It was difficult to meet locals at first and she would ask other women with children to come home and have a pie. One day a mother agreed and she broke the ice.

Daniel Salzmann who was born in Geneva and grew up in Morocco has become Mr Culture in Crans-Montana with the establishment of the Pierre Arnaud foundation - an exhibition space and Caprices the rock and pop festival. Salzmann showed an early interest in art when as a teenager he organized his first exhibition of paintings for friends.

Chapter 1. Architecture

The urban architecture in Crans-Montana is striking because of the interaction between the contrasting styles which grew from three directions. In Montana, there were the huge flat roofed TB clinics with large balconies to accommodate the beds of the sunbathing patients. The Bernese and the Bella Lui clinics are good examples. While in Crans, the modernist style of Bauhaus predominated.

Then post-modern architecture heralded by the Supercrans tower, Résidence Les Mischabels and the tour de force in the 1970s of the hotel Crans Ambassador. This all happened against the background of the standard jumbo chalets with wooden balconies.

In a leisurely walk from the funicular station to Crans which should take about an hour most of the buildings are visible. The Bernese clinic which is on the right is the first you will see. It is surrounded by a park which is a usual feature of the clinics. Continue along the Av. de la Gare and at the roundabout follow the sign to Crans.

As you walk along route du Rawyl, you will be able to see on your right the Crans Ambassador hotel and then the hotel Bella

Lui. On your left perched on a hill is the oldest hotel, hotel du Parc which was built in the 19th century. Continue along route du Rawyl and you will enter Crans.

Follow the road down and you will enter Rue Centrale. This is the area of modernism which is characterized by flat roofs, minimal decoration, with geometrical and functional lines and the use of reinforced

Le Farinet (below)

concrete and large glass windows. At the roundabout return up Rue du Prado. Here you will find more examples of Modernism and a big surprise - a huge painted bronze statue of a French Bulldog by Julien Marinetti.

All the buildings mentioned have been selected by Swiss Heritage (Patrimoine Suisse), a non-profit association that protects the heritage of urban and rural spaces. Further details and examples are given below:

Supercrans tower (1963-9) is a 19-storey building which stands high above the resort with a commanding view of the Rhone valley below and its fan shape allows maximum sunshine. It was designed by Jean-Marie Ellenberger, an architect

from Bern who trained with Corbusier. He came to Crans-Montana after World War II for treatment of tuberculosis and stayed to build the Bern sanatorium (1949), the Crans chapel (1951), among other buildings.

Due to its height and multicolored blinds, it is a symbol that can be seen from a great distance. However, nowadays the Résidences Kandahar (1960-78) also selected by Swiss Heritage are more prominent from the valley and often mistaken for the Supercrans tower.

Résidences Les Michabels (1964), an apartment block designed by Maurice Cailler and Pierre Merminod of Geneva is another exceptional building in the resort. At first glance, the striking feature is the chimneys which arise from one side of the peaked roof with its white cornices. Another feature is the positioning of the building which seems to shoot up like a tree from the unleveled site.

The biggest surprise comes when one moves away from the solid wall and around the building. Suddenly there is a mass of balconies which face the panoramic view. They are made of large plates of glass giving the illusion that they are windows even when the blinds are drawn.

The Crans Ambassador hotel (1971-2) which was designed by Claude Besse of Lens is an exciting addition to the skyline of the resort because it mimics gigantic trees. Dynamic glass facade which is enhanced through the use of colored sun protection.

The Bella Lui hotel also received the International Council on Monuments and Sites (ICOMOS) award for the preservation and restoration of large parts of the original structure. A prominent example of modernism, the hotel was originally built as a luxury sanatorium in 1929. It was designed by Rudolf and Flora Steiger-Crawford who was the first certified woman architect in Switzerland. She developed a new approach to room design with her gray-green fittings which included closets, vanity cabinets and office furniture with rolling shutters. Another similar modernist building for a TB clinic was Alvar Aalto's Paimio sanatorium in Finland which was a huge project in comparison.

Guests at the hotel can still experience the original design concept as the public areas and one room has been kept with furniture and decoration of 1930.

"It is remarkable because all the furniture in the rooms are movable as they are fitted with casters," said Rahel Isenschmied, manager of the hotel, "so items can be decontaminated underneath. Even the bed has castors. There was enough space on the balcony for it to be wheeled on lengthwise."

"The use of concrete and iron pillars in the building of Bella Lui makes it possible to have maximum light," said Rahel. "Even the corridor to the rooms on the north-facing side is bright. The Bella Lui was the first public building in Switzerland to use this modern technique. "

In fact, many tenets of Le Courbusier's pioneering ideas for modernist architecture are used at the Bella Lui such as ribbon windows, roof terraces and machine aesthetics. As patients would be there for long periods, sometimes for years, there was a distinct social atmosphere among staff and patients.

The public areas were also open to views onto the terraces as well as to the reception and entrance so patients could check on what was happening. Healthier patients and those without balconies could go and lie on sunloungers on the sun deck at the top of the building.

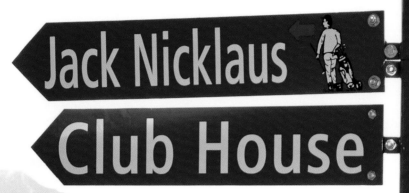

Jack Nicklaus

Club House

Caddy Master

Vestiaires

Chapter 2. Golf

Opportunity of a lifetime

Crans-Montana is a golfing paradise and you are spoilt for choice as there is something for everyone. There is the prestigious Crans-sur-Sierre Golf Club which is over a century old and offers a choice of playing on the 18-hole Severiano Ballesteros or the 9-hole Jack Nicklaus. For beginners without a handicap, they have an option of the Supercrans green above the resort or at Noas below in Chermignon.

The Golf Academy allows golfers to improve their game and enables them to play during winter on golf courses worldwide. (See separate entry). There is even an opportunity for children to be introduced to the game from the ages of 6 to 9 or have golf lessons from the ages 9 to 15. Visitors who see golf as fun and not as a sport can play at the two mini-golf courses.

Omega time

"I love Crans-Montana because once you're off the course," said Stephen Urquhart, president of Omega SA which sponsors the Omega European Masters Tournament, "you're right in the middle of the village with shops, hotels and restaurants. It's unique unlike most golf courses where off the course, you're in the middle of nowhere. Today, over the four days of golf you'll have 50,000 spectators. I can't think of another tournament on the continent which attracts so much interest."

"What I like about the tournament too is that it has history," he continued. "It has been played at the same golf club for over 70 years. The locals, most significantly Gaston Barras have stuck to the event through thick and thin which is impressive. Hats off to them!"

Some hotels are actually next to the different holes or adjacent to the courses. The Grand Hotel Golf & Palace which is official hotel for the Omega European Masters Tournament is situated near 16-hole and next to the tee off for 17-hole. The hotel Belmont is alongside the Jack Nicklaus course and at the tee off for the first hole. Guarda Golf hotel is located on the fairway of the Jack Nicklaus course and is adjacent to Severiano Ballesteros course.

The clubhouse for the Crans-sur-Sierre Golf Club is called the Sporting Club and located on the famous shopping street Rue du Prado 24. It has a terrace which

overlooks the Severiano Ballesteros course as well as a restaurant.

The Omega European Masters Tournament which is played on the Crans-sur-Sierre Golf Course early in September is the Swiss stop on the professional men's European tour and second to the British Open. Another international tournament which is also played on the course in June is the Olivier Barras Memorial for professional and amateur golfers.

"I've played with many World Number One golfers including Greg Norman and Rory McIlroy," said Stephen Urquhart who has a handicap of 15, "and enjoyed the experience. It does mean though that they hit the ball five times while I have to hit it 20 times. Mostly I like playing with people whose company I like."

To play at the 18-hole Severiano Ballesteros is a once in a lifetime experience. All the top players such as Dai Rees, Harold Henning, Sam Snead, Jack Nicklaus, Ian Woosnam, Seve Ballesteros, among others have been on the course. But what a momentous experience to stand at 7-hole tee box, breathing in the crystal clear air with the spectacular view of the ten peaks and straight ahead is the Weisshorn, the diamond of the Valais.

Golf spawned tourism

The goddess of tourism, as Pierre Ducrey aptly terms it, smiled brightly on Crans after the British opened the 9-hole golf course back in 1906. A new society was formed around the golf club. Some locals aspired to the social graces of the game,

others benefited economically. In the next five decades the burgeoning of the hotel industry went hand in hand with golf. At one end of the economic scale, there were the caddies who in the majority of cases were the valuable financial support of their families. At the other end, there were the wealthy and influential owners of the hotels who had become top players.

Olivier Barras was a member of this upper middle class and became not only the best amateur golfer in Switzerland but a 'James Dean' figure in Crans. Like the Hollywood actor, he had a penchant for fast cars and he and his friends raced against each other in their Lotus cars which were used in F1 races. He died in a crash on the Monza racing circuit in 1964 testing the Lotus of one of his friends.

Property boom

The property boom began in the late 1950s and early 1960s. The Frenchman André Jameson obtained the permission before World War II to build the first chalet on the Crans golf course. The land prices never stopped rising from then on from CHF 5 to 10 per square metre to CHF 40 and today it is around CHF 3,000. Property was opened to all comers who had land to sell. Gaston Barras was the first to establish a real estate company. (See separate entry) He used all his efforts to promote Crans as a golf mecca at the same time.

Golf Academy

If you want to surprise your friends next season, you can improve your golf handicap at the Academy of the Crans-sur-Sierre Golf Club. It is quite popular to train over the winter and it is best to book beforehand.

The Academy is one of the largest in the Alps and offers four golf options. There is a simulator which enables you to play on 43 golf courses including the Severiano Ballesteros course in Crans-Montana. The mobile platform simulates the ground slope and the graphics make it possible to play in a realistic way. There are two launch monitors - easy to use and suitable for all players to analyze golf shots on a target situated in the driving range. The artificial green provides you with a realistic surface to train your putt. The Pro area which is separated from the rest is sound-proofed and includes a launch monitor with a power platform, video biomechanics analysis and a training putting system.

From l. to r. Seve Ballesteros, Gaston Barras

This is a convenient facility to come up to speed if you are rusty or a beginner or just want to warm-up beforehand. Otherwise follow Colin Montgomerie's example and warm-up before a game at the nets in Alex Sports.

In addition, there is also a driving range where golfers can practice their swing. Adam Scott the Australian professional golfer who won the Masters Tournament in 2013 used the range in preparation for the Open and found it to his liking.

Golfers á la Crans
Mr Golf

Gaston Barras is a man of many talents, a Renaissance man. He has had several careers and is a founder of many things as well as a promoter. He started out as a

salesman of heating oil and then became a letting agent before turning to property development and real estate.

Among the things he founded was the magazine La Vie à Crans-Montana which he also edited; the new political party, the Gris; the Maison du Valais in Paris; the charity Nuit des Neiges; and he transformed the Swiss Open Golf Championship into the European Golf Masters Tournament. He also has a reputation as a promoter of tourism, classical music and golf. But it is easier to reduce his achievements in size and recognize one only. That is why he is known as Mr Golf.

Gaston Barras started from humble beginnings. He was born in the Av. de la Gare in Montana - a place he despises today, in a house without electricity, running water or heating. His father, Victorin, was a cheesemaker and had a dairy in the avenue. When he opened a second dairy in Crans, the family settled there. The house was a 100 metres from the golf course and Gaston was golf-struck. He became a caddy at the age of 7 and was in seventh heaven when he carried the golf bag of one of the 1939 Swiss Open players and later, caddied for the father of the King of Spain, Comte de Barcelona.

But then he was unaware of what fate had in store for him. He would meet many famous people including the Kennedy family, the astronaut Gene Cernin, Jean-Paul Belmondo and many top golfers such as Sam Snead, Nick Faldo, Greg Norman, Seve Ballesteros, Jack Nicklaus, among others. He grew up to be a sportsman and played ice hockey, golf and skied. After he graduated from the commercial school, he earned a living as a salesman in Lausanne and Geneva. But he always kept up with ice hockey and golf.

When he returned to Crans, he cut his teeth in real estate when he let a chalet for 15 days at CHF 180 and made a 8% commission on the deal. In 1959 he built his first property, "La Residence" which still houses Agence Barras. From 1964 and for 20 years, he was president of Chermignon commune. He had plunged into local politics because the two local political parties were always at loggerheads. So he created a new party which was aloof and stayed out of the conflicts between the other two.

In 1982, he launched La Vie à Crans-Montana. He had been traveling in the US with his son, François and they had seen a lifestyle magazine, Palm Springs Life. It triggered the idea of publishing a similar one for Crans-Montana. La Vie à Crans-Montana has succeeded brilliantly on two counts. It has proved to be a good resource on Crans-Montana and has given recognition to the British heritage as it is bilingual - French and English.

But if there is a cause which has always been close to his heart, it is golf of which he has been a tireless promoter. He joined the Crans-sur-Sierre Golf Club in 1954 and became its president in 1981. He made other contributions to golfing including the Swiss Golf Association of which he was president for six years, the creation of the Rotary European Golf Association and the European Masters which is the most prestigious golf tournament after the British Open.

In 2000, he won the coveted Swiss Sports Promoter of the year award for his unstinting creativity.

"I wanted to make golf the driving force behind tourism," he said in his acceptance speech, "in harmony with agricultural and ecological needs. And to give the Swiss who wish to participate in the sport, the possibility of playing by putting it within everyone's means."

Will he retire? No way! In his eighties, an hour sleep in the afternoon and the whiff of the Caviar House aroma keeps him invigorated. (His apartment is above the shop.)

Saint Rita comes to the rescue

Fabrice Rey who is a banker is the treasurer of the Crans-sur-Sierre Golf Club. He began as a caddy a couple of decades ago. The group would sit patiently at the club and wait until one of them was called to caddy.

"The golf club in Crans is an institution and was founded in 1906," he said. "To date, we have 1,600 members and 150 juniors. Our director is Eric Besse who comes from France. We focus on the Academy where golfers can improve their performance and play golf throughout the winter. The Olivier Barras memorial tournament is an opportunity for young players to show their mettle. Among the up and coming juniors are included Fanny Vuignier from

Sion and Damian Ulrich who won it twice and is now a Swiss Professional golfer.

The Crans-sur-Sierre Golf Club which is known worldwide has had a line of strong presidents. Sir Henry Lunn was the first to trumpet the advantages to the British of playing at the highest golf course in the world at the beginning of the 20th century. The baton was later taken up by René Payot who was president for 40 years and gained a reputation during World War II through Swiss radio in broadcasts to France as being the voice of liberty.

Then it was Gaston Barras's turn to take the baton in 1981. He also promoted golf internationally and became known as Mr Golf of Switzerland. Whenever he met people he would always hand them a sticker of the club.

"At the 2013 Golf Club Gala dinner, it was an emotional moment for Gaston Barras," said Fabrice Rey. "For he who had handed out countless pewter tankards was handed one himself for being 50 years on the committee."

Fabrice Rey marvels over the behaviour of the young who play golf compared to the young who play football. The golfers respect each other and act like gentlemen whereas the footballers are known for their rowdiness.

"Sometimes, I would sit at meetings with Gaston and tell him we need extra funds," said Fabrice Rey. "He would laugh and throw up his arms. 'I'll ask Saint Rita,' he replied.' She is the saint for impossible

From l. to r. Muriel Schindler, Samuel Bonvin

cases.'"

Golf and skiing combo

Samuel Bonvin is the Captain of the Crans-sur-Sierre Golf Club at the young age of 34. But one expects such developments from a prestigious club which has also elected four young members on the committee. He is the ideal choice because

he is an excellent golfer with a handicap of 6.6 and grew up with golf. He began playing at 8 years old and comes from a family of golfers.

"One of the problems I had as a player was my tallness," said Samuel who is 6ft 3in. "Due to my height, I needed to have custom made clubs. But since then the price of equipment has reduced radically which means that more people can afford to play nowadays."

He has overall responsibility for the club with a large membership of some 1,750. A new development is the introduction of water hazards at 10, 12 and 13-holes.

Samuel has a busy schedule because he divides his time between the club and his work at an aluminum company where he is a mechanical engineer. The only time he can spare to play is the two hours he spends with new members in their introduction to the club. He always has the same reaction of complete surprise when they come to 7-hole.

"The view is eye-catching as you can see the peaks of a lot of mountains," said Samuel, "and you don't have to go to the top of a mountain to see such an impressive sight. You just have a game of golf."

Samuel also has the invaluable experience of being a starter with the Omega European Masters Tournament. Among his duties are issuing score cards to the players, providing course information such as the pin position and the local rules. He also announces the player's name and the country they represented.

"It is interesting experience," he said. "One of the anecdotes concerns the players who have never seen snow. They are stunned when I tell them that in December the golf course is covered in 2 to 3 metres of snow."

Many players too are unaware that in win-

ter the golf club turns into a skiing area for beginners. There is a small ski lift at the Academy which takes skiers to the driving range and then another lift takes them onto the buvette in the middle of 9-hole.

"As part of our programme for the future generation of golfers," said Samuel, "we offer students at local schools an introduction to the game by providing them with a free golf Pro on the course."

Golf is my passion

Christian Barras is the scion of the prominent golfing family in Crans-Montana. His father, Gaston is known as Mr Golf and as child he had two godfathers who were golfers.

The first was Olivier Barras who was the best amateur in Switzerland - he was Swiss champion nine times, and died tragically in a car crash when he was 32 years old. (See separate entry). The second was the professional golfer, Roger Barras, who when Christian was a boy always gave him golf-related presents for Christmas and his birthdays. His favorite was the putting game in which you shot a ball into a hole.

"I started to play golf at the age of 14," he said, "but nowadays children start at ages 7 or 8. Besides the normal school curriculum, I also went to the caddy school which was located next to the Crans-sur-Sierre golf club. The term ran from July to August and 40-50 caddies from ages 7 to 14 attended. We were taught rules of behaviour to clients."

During the golfing season, the boys were

called out to do caddying. There were two categories which was based on ability and they were paid accordingly. For those in category 1, they earned CHF 6 and CHF 4 for a tip during 18 holes. In category 2, they were paid less. The whole vocation of caddying has changed with the introduction of electric golf carts.

Nowadays, caddies are only used during tournaments like the Omega European Masters when professional players are obliged by the rules to engage them. Some caddies so enjoy their vocation that they continue into adulthood.

Christian in spite of his golf handicap of

20, has excelled in other areas of golf. He signed up two American players before they won major tournaments. The first was Larry Mize who won the 1987 Masters Tournament which was his only major title. In a tie with Greg Norman and Seve Ballesteros after four rounds, Larry made a career defining shot. It was a chip from off the green at the 11-hole at Augusta to win the playoff.

The other was Scott Simpson in the same year before he won the U.S. Open - his only major title. He birdied the 14, 15 and 16-holes to overtake Tom Watson by one stroke.

"Golf is my passion," he said. "One of my memorable golf moments was to see Seve Ballesteros win the British Open in 1979 with a closing 70. He hit his tee shot into a car park on the 16-hole and yet still made a birdie with a shot I didn't think was possible. Another memorable moment was when I was in charge of entertaining players and their wives. I took Gary Player and his friend the New Zealander, Sir Bob Charles up to the Plaine Morte where they had a snow fight. Sir Bob was a successful left-handed golfer who was the first lefty to win a golf major."

Christian who runs a successful real estate business with his father is also a keen genealogist. (See Property services). His grandmother was a Rey twice over and he traced some of the descendants. One was Lucy Rey whose portrait was painted by Raphy Dallèves.

"I am interested in where we came from, where we go and where we are," he said. "Lucy's husband, Victor and her were cousins and they had a daughter Odette. Victor was a colleague of César Ritz and ran the Ritz hotel in Paris. He was the grandson of the only Conseil d'etat of Chermignon.(1847- 51) who had five children. Of the three in the next generation that emigrated to Monaco, one ended up running the Baur au Lac hotel in Zurich, another the Hotel Trianon in Versailles

From l.to r. Christian Barras, Adam Scott

and the third, Jean-Charles Rey married Princess Antoinette, the sister of Prince Rainier of Monaco.

He is also related to the Swiss politician, Micheline Calmy-Rey through his great grandfather, Louis Rey. He was the first person who was granted a license in 1907 to sell food and drinks in a buvette which was near the hotel du Golf and then later

on the 15th tee. Unfortunately, he was kicked to death by a mule in 1909. His brother Joseph had several children, one was Charles who is the father of Micheline Calmy-Rey. There is also the link with the French side of the family Barras who came to Chermignon in 1255.

Christian has also played a part in the musical life of Crans-Montana through the

Semaines Musicales de Crans-Montana where he met Rostropovich among other musicians. Now he is President of the Friends of Crans-Montana Classics.

He met his Armenian wife, Linda, at a charity event. He was supposed to be at a table with people who cancelled at the last moment. By chance he was directed to another table where she was seated. They

women players like the American Patty Berg who founded the Ladies Professional Golfers Association (LPGA) and French golfer Lally de Saint-Sauveur were fêted at the club. In 1981 the ladies section was created at the club mainly through the impetus of Béatrice 'Poupy' de Courten.

"My main responsibility is to create a programme for the whole season as we

Sporting club terrace
have two daughters.

Ladies too!

Muriel Schindler-de Sury is the Captain of the ladies section of the Crans-sur-Sierre Golf Club. Women have featured as players right from the start of golf in Crans over 100 years ago either in combined matches with men or on their own. Top

play every Tuesday and to encourage participation in the game," said Muriel. "Some members think that I am too lenient by allowing players with high handicaps to join. But I tell them that for the more talented and ambitious players they will always find challenges in competitions like inter clubs. Recently, I was pleased because I had a triumph when a golfer who started with 27 lowered it to 19 and she's getting better all the time. I also discovered a young player of 12 who already has a handicap of 15."

There are several special highlights during the year. The Ladies Trophy in the first week of June which is a popular event and attracts some 120 players from Switzerland and abroad in the two-day tournament.

The other tournaments include the final of Birdie-Open Ladies at Crans-sur-Sierre and the final of the Golf Ladies Classic which will be held at Wentworth Club, UK in which Swiss clubs like Geneva, Lausanne and Crans compete. Gant sponsored the uniform for the ladies section and also the Gant tournament. (See separate entry). However, it is important to maintain strict clothing rules at all matches and jeans as

well as shorts or skirts too high above the knee are banned.

Other sponsors include Oliveto restaurant (See separate entry). Golf Zone, the Pro shop in Sierre; and the insurance company, La Mobilière. The sponsors which provide prizes are good motivators for the members.

Visitors to Crans-Montana can play on the courses even for the short period of their stay. For those without handicaps, the 9-hole Jack Nicklaus course is suitable but they will require a green card to play. It is recommended and preferable to have several sessions at the Crans-sur-Sierre Golf Club's Academy where expert coaching is available. (See separate entry)

"I am proud of the splendid and enduring contribution the British made to golf in Crans, both men and women," she said, "and whenever I enter a golf club in the UK, I am overcome by the ambiance with the comfortable armchairs, trophies, golfing prints on the walls and above all the smell of history. It is important for us to remember such historical links and to forge new ones."

My idol Seve Ballesteros

"One day Seve Ballisteros was on a practice with a friend and I was caddying for him," said Steve Rey, a coach for the Swiss Golf Proteam. "He turned to his friend and asked him what he thought about his swing. The friend smiled. 'Don't ask me, ask him,' he answered and pointed to me. 'You're his idol and he knows everything about you.' It was true, I had

studied Seve's technique and knew all his habits."

Steve Rey grew up in the golf culture of Crans when everyone in the village was playing the game. Like most young boys, he started off as a caddy. It was fun because he met top players like Jack Nicklaus and Trevor Immelmann and also could be around Seve Ballesteros.

On one occasion, he went with a player who will be nameless as he drank beer every two holes. When they came to 5-hole, the player popped into the hotel and returned with a bottle of alcohol. He asked Steve whether he wanted some but he demurred as he was drinking milk. What was remarkable was that the player's skill as a golfer was not impaired because after two rounds, he was close to the lead.

"The most exciting time is during the European Masters," he said, "at the Seve Ballisteros 18-hole course. It's a big fiesta and all the top golfers are around in the hotels, restaurants and on the streets. I started playing in the European Masters at the age of 17 and hold the record as I have appeared 18 times."

"Now as a coach, I realize how important competitions are. Nothing develops a young player's game so quickly as competitions, specially those over two or more rounds. The mental element is important. Every golfer has to learn how to come back strongly in the second round after a bad first day. And he has to be able to deal with the euphoria of a good first round if he wants to perform well in the second."

In the 1993 season, he was one of a
handful of Swiss golfers who made it
onto the major European circuit, the PGA
tour. He retired as a professional in 2003
and became a coach to the Swiss amateur
golfers. Over the past two decades he has
played in several hundred tournaments
around the world and finds the 18-hole
course in Crans-Montana as one of the
best in Switzerland. Since the greens were
rebuilt, golfing is not easy anymore. They
are bumpy and the high scores in the clubhouse are the proof.

"Having a golf club up in the mountains
is incredible," he said." Everyone should
have the experience once in their life of
standing at 7-hole tee box. The view of the
ten peaks is spectacular and straight ahead
is the Weisshorn, the diamond of the Valais. Whenever, I return from a trip the first
thing I look at is the Weisshorn and then I
know I've arrived home."

3

Chapter 3. Skiing and Other Activities

Crans-Montana has one of the most beautiful slopes in the world with spectacular views. Skiing is carried out at altitudes between 3,000 m from Plaine Morte glacier to 1,500 m. The pistes are long and wide and enable skiers and snowboarders to use them safely side by side. There is a selection of slopes for all levels from beginners to competitions on a network of 140 km of marked pistes.

"Visitors can ski over the whole mountain," Philippe Magistretti, chairman of the board of CMA Lifts. "It's a big area for a single resort. We also host the World Cup every two years as well as the FIS races Super-G Ladies and European Cup Super-G Ladies."

Access to the pistes of reds and blues are easy via the four cableway stations that range along the resort. From west to east these are in Crans, both of which are in Crans, Grand Signal in Montana, Violettes near the Montana funicular and Aminona to the north east, some 10 km away. The woods above Montana are criss-crossed by red runs winding between the trees and Cry d'Err above Crans has several lifts serving blue runs down to the resort. Violettes provides access to the Plaine Morte

top station (3,000 m) with some exciting blues and the start of a long meandering red back to the resort. Lift passes valid in all sectors.

"It's a place where you can ski with your father, teenagers or your six year old," said Jean-Claude Biver chairman of Hublot's Administrative Board. "Nowadays, I don't enjoy shooting down the slopes doing 3 km in 3 minutes. I prefer to ski halfway and at 11.30 to sit on a terrace in the sun and enjoy raclette and a Fendant. You can do that in Crans-Montana when you start early. The slopes are in sun and not in the shadow and you avoid crowds which I hate when I ski." Mr Biver has an apartment in Crans-Montana. (See a separate entry).

Ecole Suisse de ski de Montana
Bâtiment Ycoor 1
Montana
027 481 85 15
info@essmontana.ch
www.essmontana.ch

The Swiss Ski School Montana which was established in 1926 has a long tradition of nurturing and teaching winter sports. Skiing has developed significantly since the world's first downhill race - the Lord

Roberts of Kandahar Challenge trophy which was held in 1911. The people of Montana went to great lengths to retain a strong connection with the British. Henri Bauer, a ski instructor even spent the next summer in London to learn English.

The Kandahar was a free-for-all with no marked pistes and the equipment was Gothic in comparison with today when Sir Arnold Lunn introduced the downhill races. Skiers wore soft, low boots and the skis had no sharp ends to cut through the snow which had not been groomed into a hard-beaten surface. The winning time was 61 minutes with a speed of 30 mph compared to 85 mph today.

The modern ski equipment is high-tech and offers many options from personal fitting boots to skis designed for different needs from Alpine to cross-country. The new sport of snowboarding has also developed as well as freestyle and free riders. It is important for example for skiers to obtain advice on ski binding adjustment to prevent knee injuries.

"We have 200 staff who can advise clients on the best equipment and skiing techniques," said Nicolas Masserey, director of the Swiss Ski School."They can also provide a quality service to fit the needs of each individual. What is important for our ski instructors is for them to win the trust of the clients and show how they can ski safely and gain pleasure from winter sports."

It is worth noting that the son of one of the ski instructors, Luca Aerni, is racing in the slalom world cup.

The ski area in Crans-Montana is essentially for the family because it caters for all levels.The resort is intermediate with a good beginner terrain. There are three short but easy runs on Plaine Morte glacier where good snow is guaranteed for beginners. The nursery slopes which are down by the golf course are easier but can quickly become worn.

On the whole, Crans-Montana is a resort of long, open cruising runs. There are four lifts which start from Aminona, Violettes Grand Signal and Crans gondola. The largest confluence of intermediate pistes is in the Violettes sector with winding trails through woods. The Toula chair leads to steeper reds and one can head down the National ski slope from Bella Lui. Both the National and the slope from Chezeron were World Cup runs. The official black run is under the Toula chair.

"Although, we are not known as an extreme ski area," said Nicolas Masserey, "our staff can still surprise skiers with off-piste areas. There are virginal places where few or no one has been."

With a guide a number of itineraries are possible for the Plaine Morte glacier. There is a descent to the lake Zeuzier which involves walking through tunnels, skiing on a summer road to reach the ski lifts of the resort of Anzere.

Crans-Montana is an active snowboarding centre and the Adrenaline snow park at the top of the Crans gondola is one of the largest in Switzerland. It has a half-pipe, several rails, an area for beginner, free-styles, a ski cross/boarder cross course and a new snow park for teenagers.

There are about 50 km of Langlauf tracks including a 10 km trail for Nordic skiers at an altitude of 3000 m on the Plaine Morte glacier. Besides skiing, the resort offers ice-skating, curling and snowshoeing.

In summer, there are three slopes for downhill mountain biking from easy levels to impressive big jumps. At weekends, the bike park which is near the Crans gondola is worth visiting as entertaining displays are given.

"Crans-Montana is balcony with incredible views," said Nicolas Masserey. "It is un-like other resorts which tend to overwhelm you with the presence of the mountains. The panorama imparts a good feeling irrespective of what sport you're involved in. And then there's the sunny plateau."

Walks

Summer excursions round Crans-Montana include areas from the Rhone valley to Plaine Morte glacier at 3000 m. A diversity of scenery can be discovered during the walks from vineyards, pine and larch forests, irrigation canals (called bisses) to mountain lakes and eternal snow on the glaciers. The paths are signposted and magnificent panoramas of the Alps are always in view.

Tips: Take a camera as there are many opportunities for photographs. The walks can be complimented by a hiking map,

Crans-Montana-Sierre, by Toporando and the website: www.crans-montana.ch/rando

An unusual approach to walking is to discover all aspects of nature, medicinal plants and animal tracks. Or walks under starlight, through breezes and winds. And even to meet the inhabitants of the mountains. The hiking guide Anne Rey offers such adventures.

Her enthusiasm stems from her childhood when she accompanied her family to pick wild spinach, lady's mantel for stomach aches and violets for treating coughs.

So if you are ready for a snowshoe walk and want to land up in the hamlet of Colombire, do not be surprised to have a raclette cooked over a wood fire followed by a downhill sledge run.

Mountain guide - herbalist
Rue de la Pavia 16
Montana-Village
079 365 82 62
anne.rey@randoplaisir.ch
www.randoplaisir.ch

In addition there is the prominent guide Liz Bestenheider who has been inter-viewed. (See separate entry).
078 602 6406

Easy walks

1. Panorama 4,000. (40-45 minutes)
Start at Chetzeron and head up to Cry d'Er towards Violettes. The path can be littered with limestones which are popular hiding places for marmots - mountain mice. The walk continues below the glacier and runs along the bisse ending at the Colombire hamlet. There you will find an eco museum, a cheesemaking museum and a restaurant. (See separate entry).

2. Grand Bisse de Lens. (2 hours +)
The walk is between the villages of Icogne and Chermignon d'en Bas. (There is another Chermignon called d'en Haut.) Start at Châtelard Hill which has the Christ the King statue at the top. Some of the rock faces along the bisse are vertigious.

3. Bisse Neuf and Bisse de Varen. (3 hours)
Start at Venthône and the path runs along the hillside, through a pine forest and a field of stones until you reach Varen which is the German-speaking part of the canton.

4. Bisse du Sillonin. (2 hours)
Start at Icogne and end at Chelin. There are several signposted options. The bisse was built at the beginning of the 15th century and irrigates meadows and vines from Planisses to Flanthey.

5. Terre de Foi. (5 hours)
The circular walk covers chapels and churches which provide evidence of the Christian faith across the communes. Start and end in Corin.

6. Chemin de Vignoble. (2 hours)
The wine route takes you through vineyards, past wineries where you can taste the indigenous wine such as Fendant, Syrah, Cornalin and Petite Arvine. There are also educational posters which explain the history. Start from Ollon to Venthône.

Moderate walks

1. Sentier de Huiton. (3 hours)
The walk along the Plaine Morte glacier (2927 m) offers spectacular views and proceeds past lakes to Les Violettes. Start at the glacier and end at Les Violettes.

2. Chemin du Soleil. (7 hours +)
The walk which runs alongside the Tsittoret bisse can be done in three sections. The first leg is from Crans to Vermala. The second leg is from Vermala to the Colombire hamlet.

The final leg which passes one of the most beautiful natural areas around the Tièche waterfalls is from the hamlet to Leukerbad, a distance of over 5 hours. Start in Crans, Vermala or Colombire hamlet.

3. Bisse de la Transhumance. (5 hours +)

The walk shows the annual migrations of the locals. It follows the paths taken to the alpage to graze the cows in the summer and then to work in the vineyards during the spring and autumn. Start at Montana and end in Colombire hamlet.

3

4. Bisse du Ro. (3 hours +)

The walk is along the bisse which was built in the middle ages and cut into a rock face. Some of the passages are vertigious and people suffering from vertigo should avoid the walk. Start from Zeurzier dam and end at Crans cableway station.

A list of guides for walking, hiking and mountain climbing is provided below.

Guided mountain walks
Route du Parc 3
Montana
027 480 44 66
info@sms04.ch
www.sms04.ch

Guided mountain walks
Impasse de la plage 3
Montana
027 480 10 10
contact@adrenatur.ch
www.adrenatur.ch

Mountain guide Bureau
Bâtiment Ycoor 1
Montana
027 481 85 15
info@essmontana.ch
www.essmontana.ch

Riding

Manège de Crans-Montana
route du Manège 3
Montana
076 335 56 76
mail@kronwall.ch

Ruedi Wallerbosch and Melany Pannatier run the most modern riding stable in the Valais. They offer a variety of lessons from beginners to dressage and show jumping.

Many locals stable their horses there including Tania Mathieu the prominent show jumper and owner-director of the International Summer Camp Montana. (See separate entry).

Her two horses, the Swiss Lupin and the German stallion, Caludis are exercised there when she is too busy to do it herself.

"Riding for an hour or so, just clears my head," said Tania who is also responsible for sports and events.

The entrance of the spacious and bright building leads into a cafe-restaurant with a terrace and view over paddocks and an indoor riding circuit. There are 33 loose boxes for the horses and Shetlands, and each is equipped according to the new laws of animal protection with a small outdoor patio. Inside within view of the cafe-restaurant is the horse walk for exercising the horses.

"Horse-riding is an addiction or disease," said Ruedi Wallerbosch who is an expert on all aspects of riding and horses. "I have owned several riding schools and seen many people being infected at an early age. But then we owe a lot to the horses. Where would civilization be without them? Just think of Alexander the Great, Napoleon and transport throughout the ages for ordinary people. There has always been a harmony between these animals and mankind."

Melany who was born in Montana, was attracted to horses at an early age and trained with Ruedi in the Solothurn area where he had a riding school. When the riding school opened in Montana, she returned to teach dressage and to manage it with Ruedi.

There is sufficient space for riding in the fields around the plateau and during winter the indoor exercising area is ideal for riding. During the summer holidays, there are training courses for children. All sorts of activities are organized with the horses in the morning as well as sports in the afternoon.

3

Chapter 4. Shopping

Shopping is one of the sports besides golf and skiing that visitors can indulge. The sunny weather and the healthy air put them in a relaxed frame of mind for shopping. Although, there are no pedestrianized areas, the traffic is limited to a quiet zone of 30 km/h and the motorists are respectful of people.

There are two shopping areas and the selection of shops is varied. It is well worth a wander from one end to the other and the celebrated Taillens - boulangerie and teashops are found at both ends.

Crans to the west, is the more upmarket with the largest luxury shopping area in the Alps. The Rue du Prado has the highest concentration of big brands and all within walking distance. You could be in Paris, London, New York or even Dubai except for the panoramic views of the Alps. Some 180 boutiques and shops for fashion, watches, jewelry, interior design, galleries, antique and craft shops as well as sport shops where you can obtain advice from professionals about the latest and most up to date equipment. This is also where you find the best hotels and restaurants but it can feel a little quiet in off-peak week season.

Montana to the east is more commercial and busy all the year round. It compliments Crans and also has a range of shops, restaurants, hotels which are well suited to families and the sporty crowd.

Crans

Concept Store Custo Barcelona

Rue du Prado 19
Crans
027 480 4345
www.athina-crans.ch
cransmontana.custo@custo-barcelona.com

Rue du Prado was changed forever when Julien Marinetti's huge bronze painted sculpture of a French bulldog was installed on the sidewalk outside the Custo Barcelona concept store. Small versions of Marinetti's sculptures can be bought inside this extraordinary shop and many passersby pop into the shop to talk about the French artist's Doggy John.

The extraordinary shop combines the art of Julien Marinetti and Custo Barcelona brand fashion as well as lots of different accessories like Mexicana, Montale, Mou Boots, Erfurt, Beck Sonder Gaard, Jeffrey

Campbell, among others. It is a true eclectic collection of clothes and accessories. It is not unusual for customers to spend hours browsing as the shop always has new stock. For example, in the shoe section there are Toms which are canvas slip-ons and have been worn by Argentinian farmers for centuries.

"We dress people from 7 to 80," said Elodie Folliot, the manager. "Popular items include the scarf collection from Denmark, the handmade bags from Ibiza and the Mexican cowboy boots. We have multiple choices and prices are from CHF 12 for little bracelets and upwards."

Gant
Rue Centrale 64
Crans

027 480 43 70
078 805 9645
crans-montana@gantstores.ch

The American sportswear brand has a store with a NH lounge-bar attached. They are one of the few stores which are open throughout the year. The range includes baby clothes - from six months to three years, clothes for boys, some household goods and usual men's and women's clothes.

"We are selling an image and the best-sellers are the Yale shirt," said Alain Kamerzin, the manager, "and the cushions with knitted coverings and stars."

Boutique Moncler
Rue du Prado 6

Crans
027 480 48 43
078 899 54 34
ch02@industries-group.com
www.moncler.com

A global brand famous for its quilted
jackets with distinctive horizontal boudins
or lines of stitching. In winter it has a total
look of gloves, hats, jumpers jackets and
shoes and in summer the look is colourful,
sporty and urban chic. Clothes for both
men and women.

"When people come into a luxury shop
such as Montcler," said Florence Mancini,
the manager, "they know what they want.
But I can help them make the right choice.
The clothes are what I call easywear."

Chopard
Rue du Prado 16
Crans
027 481 11 69

Chopard is one of the great Swiss watch
brands which was established by Louis-Ul-
ysse Chopard over 150 years ago. Since
then the company has progressed by leaps
and bounds with its introduction of L.U.C
handcrafted watches, its happy diamonds
and Haute jewelry collections. This is an
authorized dealer and the nearest boutique
is in Lausanne.

Boutique Dune
Rue Centrale 27
Crans
027 480 3882

The shop sells everyday chic clothes for
women at affordable prices. It has a comprehensive range from tops, skirts, jeans
to shoes.

Besides Dune by Dune (the boutique's
own range), there are clothes by the Italian
designer Cristina Gavioli. Her range
includes knitwear, separates, dresses,
outwear, accessories and can be arranged
in a way that will suit any customer and an
age group from 16 to 60. Among the other
selection of designers are included Corleo-
ne, La Fée Maraboutée, Stella Forest, and
Muse of love.

"It's the ideal place for women who suddenly needs a cocktail dress for an event,"
said Consuelo Paltinieri, the manager. "Or
someone who likes to accessorize because
we have a large choice of items."

Brunello Cuccinelli
Rue du Prado 10
Crans
027 481 8112

The clothes in the shop are understated
and usually the colours of a collection are
pastels like grey, white and beige. Some
people have described his clothes for men
and women as insanely nice, timeless and
beyond trends. He is big on cashmere.
The customers tend to be people who like
quality clothing but like the brand to be
incognito.

"I've worked for brands like Chanel," said
Magaly Robyr who runs the boutique.
"They attract people who like to show
everyone what trademark they are wear-
ing. There is nothing wrong with that. But
our customers are blasé about stating their

4

brand so brazenly."

Brunello Cucinelli is an Italian fashion designer who combines fashion and style with a philosophy of life. Cucinelli, the son of a factory worker, started off in business by selling coloured cashmere sweaters for women. He has reinvested most of the profits from Cucinelli cashmere in restoring his wife's hometown of Solomeo, Umbria where the company has its headquarters.

"I need to make a profit," said Cucinelli, "but I would like to do it with ethics, dignity and morals. It's my dream."

Jacky Bonvin Cigars
Rue Centrale 60
Crans
027 481 26 34
contact@cigars-bonvin.ch
www.cigars-bonvin.ch

The shop has specialized in Cuban cigars for more than 50 years and has one of the best selections of cigars and humidifiers in Switzerland. They are authorized agents for Habanos and Davidoff. Partagas, Montecristo, Romeo y Julieta, among others and specials like Upmann Sir Winston and Cohiba Beluke are always available.

The shop is unique as it offers a choice of cigars and a wide selection of books. So while the husband discusses cigars, his wife can browse in the bookshop. Besides art books, novels and non-fiction they have a good selection of golf books and, of course, English books.

The shop is named after a famous Swiss golfer from Crans-Montana, Jacky Bonvin. He was a friend of Zino Davidoff and after retiring from competitions, he developed a renowned cigar department in the bookstore with his wife Luce who was an avid reader. Their son Philippe runs the shop with his wife Patricia.

Côté Montagne
Rue Centrale 8,
Crans
027 481 8109
0794347979

Daniel Emery is a top interior decorator in town. If you are building a chalet or bought one or simply want to redecorate, this is the one-stop place to come. He will organize craftsmen and find suitable objects and furniture necessary to create an environment which you like and reflects your lifestyle.

Daniel Emery lives and works in Crans-Montana. What is fascinating is that he has the talent for decorating at his fingertips and is an autodidact.
"I started young," he said. "I wasn't very interested in school but I was motivated by textiles, creating lampshades and to the annoyance of my parents, I was continually changing the decoration in my room. I learnt my profession by visiting second-hand and antique shops."

He listens to what people want. Then he immerses himself into their lifestyle. He has described himself as a chameleon as he takes on the personality of the person or people. Recently, he flew to New York to see the home of an American couple who wanted him to decorate their apartment in the Supercrans tower.

"I estimate the size of the rooms and imagine the atmosphere," he said, "once that has been completed, the major part of my work has been accomplished. For the rest, I scour flea markets, second-hand and antique shops or modern furniture stores for the right pieces and then leave the rest to good craftsmen."

He still likes to change the decor of his home. "I have mounted several Hermes scarves in large gilded frames and change them according to my moods," he said. "I also recommend to my clients to frame old illustrations, prints or maps as they never go out of fashion."

Heritage
Watches and Jewelry,
Rue du Prado 19
Crans
027 480 4385
info@heritage-crans.ch
www.heritage-crans.ch

The shop stocks eight brands of watches including Hublot, Zenith, Ulysse Nardin, IWC Schaffhausen, Girard-Perregaux, Franck Muller, TAG Heuer and RJ-Romain-Jerome. The jewelry which compliments the watch range are Messika, Morganne Bello, Rita & Zia and Pesavento, among others. Heritage also has its own range of upscale jewelry.

Georges Grintakis who is passionate about watches, bought his first Rolex with money he had borrowed from his uncle. Besides Hublot which now has a Ferrari collection, he likes to talk about new brands. RJ-Romain Jerome, for example, has the Moon-DNA collection which incorporates metal from the Apollo XI spacecraft, Moon dust and fibres from a spacesuit worn on the International Space Station while the Titanic-DNA collection has salvaged material from the shipwreck such as rusted steel.

Franck Muller on the other hand is a watchmaker of complications. The Perpetual Calendar Bi-Retro watch has multi functions such as the day, the month and lunar phases as well as being a perpetual calendar. His watches are fun and have innovative faces including a texture of crocodile skin.

Georges established his shop in 2008 and as he knew he would spend a lot of time in it, he had a Feng Shui master to design the interior. Consequently, the shop has a pleasant atmosphere and generates calm and good energy which allows for long stays by the owner and the customer whom he has enthralled. If the customer has indulged himself with an expensive watch - they go upwards in price to CHF 100,000, then he may wish to salve his guilt by buying a trinket for his wife or mistress. The choice is colourful and delightful.

But for George, there are other challenges. "It's like a cigar smoker who one day would like to smoke a Cohiba Beluke," he said. "That's my dream."

Crans Prestige
Watches and jewelry
Rue du Prado 9,
Crans
027 481 1405

info@crans-prestige.ch
www.crans-prestige.ch

It has a range of watches including Rolex, Audemars Piguet, Panerai, Cartier, Vacheron Constantin and Breitling. The jewelry mainly comprises Italian and French brands such as Pomellato, Dodo, Albanu, Piero Milano, Dinh Van, Mattiolo and Marco Bicego.

Lara Vocat is a bright woman with a bubbly personality. She is one of the youngest managers in Rue du Prado who runs the Crans Prestige. To have achieved such a position in her early thirties required more than a pretty face and promises great things for the future. But she has already had a fascinating past. She trained in hospitality and tourism in Venice and managed three clothing boutiques in Corsica. When she arrived in Crans-Montana, she took a job as a bar woman and gained knowledge of cocktails as well as 200 brands of whiskies.

"When the position at Crans Prestige became available," she said, "I insisted with the boss that I attend the course on watches and jewelry at La Chaux de Fonds. I now have the brevet fédéral and I am professional on watches and jewelry."

Lara who is a Venetian, lives with her husband David in Randogne. When she was a child she liked to pick up shiny stones and then with the first money she earned she bought a watch.

When she first settled in Crans-Montana, she found that the people she met were a bit closed to outsiders but afterwards, they became friends. In fact her best friends are her local customers. "I'm not finished with customers when I sell a watch or jewelry to them," she said. "They appreciate that I provide an after sales service. Then I begin to build a relationship with them."

After seven years at Crans Prestige she feels at home with the iconic luxury watch brands. "Why do men have several watches?" she said. "For men, watches are jewelry. Some have collections of 100 watches."

Customers exhibited national characteristics. The Russians tend to buy the most expensive watches. The Italians go for the brands while the British and French tend towards Cartier classics.

"The Pomellato jewelry is a fun discovery," she said. "Their trademarks are rings of many colours. And the charms for their bracelets send different messages. The octopus = I want to embrace you, the dodo = I want to be your lover and the dog = I want to be your friend."

Lorenz Bach
Rue du Prado 18
Crans.
027 4781 81 10
(See entry in Montana.)

Alex Sports
Rue du Prado 31
Crans
027 481 40 61
contact@alexsports.ch
www.alexsports.ch

One of the jaw-dropping experiences in Crans is to visit Alex Sports because the selection and colours of sportswear is incredible. It ranges from shoes and clothing for golf wear, football, tennis, hiking, cycling to skiing outfits but also the equipment that goes with it. Even people who are not into sports will find something stylish to wear such as a long sleeve sports shirt for formal wear. Big brands for ski, golf and outdoor wear like Kjus and Bogner and in the Pro Shop, golf clubs, balls and equipment like Titleist, TaylorMade and Callaway.

Custom-made equipment can be ordered in the Pro shop. For example, handmade skis not only increase performance but keep their elasticity longer. They lose about 3% over 90 days compared to ordinary skis which lose some 30% after 30 days. Hand-fitted ski boots and sport shoes and maintenance of skis is also available. Custom-made also applies to golf clubs with the head, shaft and flex. Rentals are available on all equipment and cycles.

Alex sports is on both sides of Rue du Prado and connected by a tunnel. It consists of five shops and includes the main store, Kjus, Odlo and Cry d'Err. The selection in the main store includes boutiques for men, women, sports and town shoes and the Scotch House.

"What is important for me is that each customer is different in his or her needs," said Alex Barras, who is the third generation to run the business. "When I or my team serve them, we always think from their perspective. We put ourselves in their shoes. Before they select an item, be it clothing or equipment, we ask what makes them happy in that sport."

Alex Barras is proud that they have opened the world's first solo Kjus shop. "The fashion style is impeccable and the clothes are from quality fabrics," he said. "The down jackets are incredible because they are not only ultra light and functional but delicate and chic in appearance."

Lasse Kjus, a Norwegian was a World Cup skiing champion three times and an Olympic champion. He established a skiwear brand over a decade ago which later extended to golf and outdoor wear.

It is little wonder that of the visitors in winter only 40% are skiers, the rest are into the sport of shopping. But what is 'le must' is Alex Sports where the selection of fashion and functional clothes, shoes and sports equipment is outstanding.

Montana

Lorenz Bach
Rue Louis Antille 4
Montana
027 47812733
www.lorenzbach.com

There are two Lorenz Bach shops. One is in Montana and the other in Crans and none of them have the same stock. So if you are into these clothes, it is best to go to both and see the ranges.

"What's in the window is different from what you'll find inside," said François Gervais, the manager. "There's always a

Alex Barras

surprise and on one occasion there was
a variation of the Sgt Pepper's Lone-
ly Hearts Band uniforms. On another
there were towels to match the bathing
costumes. Whatever, there are enough
different clothes to please the tastes of
many people."

Lorenz Bach who is from Gstaad started out with a ski shop, Silver Sport in

Rougemont Gstaad. But he had always
been interested in fashion as a boy. He
opened his first shop under his own label
in 1986. His style was to inject a flush of
colours into a trendy selection of luxury
clothes. It is a top alpine-chic brand and
became a hit amongst the ski resort crowd
who wanted something flashy but not
necessary a big brand. Swiss quality and
the small red cross stitch is the distinctive

feature on Lorenz Bach clothes.

"My clothes are comfortable," he said," and the different colours can be worn together in combinations. Men from the age of 20 onwards can wear my clothes and look sportive. The same applies to women from the age of 20 onwards can wear my clothes and look attractive."

Yet Bach's own label lives happily amongst plenty of other luxury brands like Roberto Cavalli, Ralph Lauren and Etro.

Au Bonheur des Dames
Rue Louis Antille 1
Montana
027 481 4434
079 431 2809
mbramaz@bluewin.ch
www.aubonheurdesdames.ch

Emile Zola wrote a novel called Au Bonheur des Dames or Ladies' Delight based on the department store in Paris, Le Bon Marché. In the centre of Crans-Montana, you find a bijou boutique with a similar aim to enchant women with its range of household items, fabrics and gifts.

The popular products are a large range of scented candles to infuse your home with the aromas you love and make you smile. The candles are handmade with natural aromas and as they are in glass jars they also make nice gifts. A pride of place is given to a huge silver bowl of wax candles which can be converted into a container for a jeroboam of champagne.

Other popular items include throws which can be draped over settees or used as bedspreads. They come in a wide collection of faux fur, wool, alpaca etc. Smaller gifts are furry, rabbit skin pompoms or hearts to decorate keychains.

Besides the gifts, lighting, furniture and household items, there is showroom with fabrics for curtains, cushions, tablecloths, blankets which can be custom-made. The interior decoration of the hotel rooms in Chetzeron have been done by Michèle Bramaz, the owner. (See separate entry). She once worked in a bank but always had the desire to open a boutique with things that would delight ladies in their homes. She fulfilled her wish in 1998.

La Frileuse
Av. de la Gare 12
Montana
027481 2520
info@lafrileuse.ch
www.lafrileuse.ch

The lingerie shop has a comprehensive range of Swiss cotton underwear like Hanro, Zimmerli and Callida as well as French designer wear like Aubade and Lise Charmel.

"It's interesting how the fashions have changed," said Marielle Clivaz-Ketteridge, the owner. "When I was a girl, the ranges and colours of underwear were very limited. Now there is bigger selection and the latest development in women's underwear after the thong is the shorty."

David L'Instant Chocolat
Av. de la Gare 6
Montana
027 481 45 12

instant-chocolat.ch
david@instant-chocolat.ch

Chocoholics should make a beeline for the shop as as soon as they arrive. The selection is so varied with subtle ganaches that melt on the tongue that they will want to taste everything during their stay. Flavours right across the board from pineapple puree, old Jamaica rum to caramel fondant with lemon to passion fruit jelly and white chocolate filling with yogurt. The ganaches are colourful too with reds of raspberry, calamansi or pink pepper; deep blue of blackcurrants; yellows of lemon from Menton; and whites of coconut and Matcha tea.

Specialities include truffle, choconougat and artistic chocolate creations made for festivals like Easter and Christmas, birthdays or special occasions.

"The key to making a good truffle is to balance the taste of chocolate with the other ingredients in the filling," said David Pasquiet. "When you eat the truffle, you should close your eyes and be able to discern each taste in turn."

The highest quality of ingredients are used and for customers who know the health benefits of a daily dosage of 10 gm of flavanoids, there is Aticoa with 63% cocoa.

"Some of our chocolates like the choconougat are so popular," said his wife Virginie, "that we Fedexed 1,000 pieces twice for weddings in the Middle East."

Avalanche
Rue Antille 15
Montana
027 480 2424
info@avalancheshop.com
www.avalancheshop.com

Dave Albrecht's Avalanche Pro Shop is where the action is for specialists - cycling, snowboarding and mountain biking. He opened the shop 16 years ago and has seen it, done it and been there.

"Gear is personal," he said. "We can supply it all or just bits."

Brands sold: Anon, Burton, Bixs, Commercial, Camelback, Dakine, Deuter, EVOC, Earlyrider, FiveTen, GoPro, Helly Hansen,Intense Cycles, IXS, Isostar, Libteck, Park Tools, Quiksilver, Roxy, Spank, Troy Lee Designs, Volcom, Vans, Yeti Bikes.

Renting: Bikes, snowboards, skis, telemark.
Additional service: Repairs for all brands, bikes, skis, snowboards.

Swissrent a sport
Rue Louis Antille 14
Montana
027 481 00 77
Rte des Barzettes 1
Montana
027 480 49 81
www. swissrent-montana.ch

Equipment rental and ski-service. They will come to your hotel to fit the equipment.

Stöckli, Salomon and Atomic skis, trousers, jackets, gloves and helmets.

Zermatten-Sports SA
Rote de Monte Sano 2
Montana
027 481 18 41
www.zermattensports.ch

Other shops are located near the Télécabine du Grand Signal and in the resort of Aminona. They both provide a renting service for all your skiing requirements. A maintenance and repair service is also available at both sites.

Galleries

Caroline Dechamby
Rue du Prado 1
Crans
027 481 68 08
virginie@caroline-dechamby.com
www.caroline-dechamby.com

Caroline Dechamby is a Dutch artist who is Valaisian by adoption. She has a pop style and has her name emblazoned on the building of her modern gallery of three floors filled with her artworks.

Caroline is prolific - currently into plexiglass installations and went from flower painting into erotic (it was a challenge), Mise en scène, Caméléon, La reine, Diamants, Graffiti's and Monochromes.

"All buyers of my works feel the energy in them," said Caroline. "Painting is like meditation, I have a sense of balance and I'm communicating with the vertical. You have to be disciplined and if I miss a day

then I have to make it up the next."

Caroline grew up in Utrecht where both her parents were in creative occupations. Her father was an architect and her mother a painter. If she had a mentor it would be Magritte because she too has a sense of humour and likes blue skies. Her mother painted Magritte's dove motif on the wall of her bedroom and she remembers being fascinated by it.

"Whenever I've been through crises in my life," said Caroline, "something that really turns your stomach, I've always persisted with my painting. It was my mother's advice and she added that 'one day, another world will open for you."

And look how the art world has opened! She even has designed lamps and has a line of watches.

Tornabuoni Gallery
Rue Centrale 5,
Crans
Crans-Montana
027 481 2050
www.tornabuoniart.fr

The top gallery which has branches in Florence, Milan and Paris specializes in Italian artists from Futurism, Arte Povera and Transavantguardia to international movements such as abstractionism and informal art and contemporary experiments that no longer have geographic borders.

"One of my favorite artists is Lucio Fontana," said Michele Casamonti, owner of the gallery. "Fontana invented the concept of spatialism which brought three-dimensionality into canvas. He treated canvas like a sculpture. He changed the history of art."

This is a reference to Fontana's slash series from 1949 which consisted in slashes or holes on the surface of monochrome paintings which he named art for the Space Age. He gives them a sense of illusion and depth through having a black backing to the canvas.

"But it's important to get the line from Fontana to other big names in Italian art of the second half of the 20th century," he said. "They include Alighiero Boetti, Enrico Castellani, Piero Manzoni, Arnaldo Pomodoro and Alberto Burri, among others. Boetti's incomparable world map has provided a modern role for tapestry through the portrayal of flags of nations at a given time in history."

At the Crans-Montana gallery he has a special room dedicated to young Italian artists. Here he has selected artists of the future such as Malipiero and Benetta.

"This is one of the most interesting aspects of my work," he said. "A good gallerist has to be ten years ahead of his time. I'm like a surfer who wants to spot a wave when it's piccolo, just beginning to build. To do that 50% is based on experience and knowledge and the other 50% on instinct. You have to have a nose for art when you go to an artist's studio and see his work. It is one thing to buy a painting for 10,000 euros and after 10 years, it has doubled in value. And another when the 10,000 euros has become 100,000 euros."

Galerie d'Art Annie
Les Vignettes
Route de Rawyl 45
Montana
027 481 1384
079 691 5166
robyrannie@netplus.ch

Annie Robyr opened the first art gallery in the resort in 1970. It is a small space on two floors, well lit and has a wooden cabin as a office. She is proud of the many artists she has exhibited over the years. They include Hans Erni whose mural decorates the foyer of the Bern Clinic in Montana, Andre Bucher who made the special handrails of the staircase in her gallery and Mizette Putallaz who was exhibited at Gianadda in 1991 and liked to use white in her calm compositions.

Other works represented in her gallery are of the Valasian painter Chavaz, the Italian surrealist Pier Enrico Guzzi, the Italian sculptor Massimo Villani who has a single wooden piece and another Valaisian painter François Pont who lives and works in London.

"I showed G. Borgeaud before Gianadda did," she said, "and he gave me sound advice. 'Trust your instinct and don't listen to anyone.' I was born to share beautiful things. I have a feeling for what people like and help them free themselves of their outside shell.'"

In keeping with her love of beautiful things, she also has a small collection of the Norwegian designer Oleana who creates clothes from alpaca and wool silk mixtures.

Chapter 5. People

The Valais has always been an isolated canton, in particular the mountain villages where the oldest inhabitants are reputed to be the wind and jealousy. To obtain an insider's view into the culture, you have to see beyond the landscape, the buildings and into the hearts of the people. Interviews have been conducted with the locals as well as the foreign friends who inter-married, live in the resort or are simply in love with the place.

Born and bred

THE VISIONARY

Francis Clivaz was born in Bluche when it was a hamlet of the Randogne commune. Today it is synonymous with Les Roches, the International School of Hotel Management. (See separate entry). It is incredible because his family had a hand in founding it! The story perfectly illustrates the fact that anyone from a small village who has a vision can become part of the global village.

Francis and his four brothers grew up in the hamlet and helped on the ancestral farm. "Like other boys, we milked the cows," said Francis. "In summer we took them up to the alpage and brought them down in winter. In the spring and autumn we worked in the vineyards."

But the Clivazs were different from the other families. Francis' father ran the local post office. The fact alone changed the life of the boys because from an early age, they were exposed to different cultures. So it was natural for them accept differences in language, culture, religion and race. They became open to people from all over the world.

Sir Anthony Eden

During World War II, the composer and musician Paul Hindemith fled from the Nazis and took a chalet in Bluche. "We became friends with him and his wife," said Francis. "Another person we met was Sir Anthony Eden, Prime Minister of the UK who came to stay in our chalet. He had wanted a holiday in a remote, quiet place. Then after World War II we found that Chalet Soleil, the former home of Elizabeth von Arnim was a refuge run by nuns for tubercular young women."

In 1952-3, Francis' oldest brother Marcel organised a ski camp and in the next year, together with another brother, Jean-Pierre, they established a private school, Ecole des Roches, which taught subjects in English. At the time there were over 200 private schools in Switzerland, most of them finishing schools for young girls who were taught to be ladies. The Ecole des Roches prepared students for their Matura or Baccalaureate and attracted students from Italy and France. Later in 1959, when US companies set-up their headquarters in Geneva, American children were bussed over from the city. When the enrollment of students had risen to 220 from 60 different countries, the two other brothers, Roger and Francis joined the family team.

"In 1979, we realized that there was a big demand for hospitality schools," he said, "and the only two in Switzerland, Ecole Hôtelière Lausanne and Glion, taught in French. We then changed the objective of the Ecole and founded Les Roches Hotel and Tourism School." It was the beginning of a great success worldwide.

The Fire
When Les Roches was destroyed by fire in April 1985, the family team acted quickly to minimise disruption to the curriculum. Within 48 hours arrangements were made to house the students and transfer teaching facilities to three hotels in Montana. Construction of the new buildings began in May 1986 and the school moved into its new buildings in June 1987. In 2000, Les Roches school of hotel management was accredited by the Swiss Cantonal authorities to teach bachelor and master degrees. The degrees of Bachelor of Business Administration in International Hotel Management and Master in Business

Administration in Hospitality Management are also recognized by the New England Association of schools and colleges. Today, there are 2,500 students on the Les Roches campus and it is by far the largest enterprise in the Valais. It is now part of the Laureate International Universities.

Francis had vision and soon had the opportunity of establishing his own international school. "One day, my brothers rang me," he said, "and asked if I wanted to start my own business. At the time I was managing a hotel in Geneva. I agreed and that is how I established the College du Léman International School in May 1960. The American students no longer needed to be bussed to Crans-Montana as they came to my school."

Today the College du Léman is the flagship of the Meritas Family of Schools and has 2,250 students. Francis Clivaz is still associated with Glion and Les Roches where he is a member of the Governing Board and President of College du Léman. He travels the world and attends Alumni functions. He received international honors from Endicott College, Boston and is an honorary member of the board of trustees of New England Association of colleges and schools, Boston, of the European Council of International Schools, London and of the Hostellerie Swiss, Bern.

"Our schools are significant inasmuch as we prepare young men and women in the best way for their futures," he said. "Besides educating them, we also give them codes of behaviour, the acceptance of authority, discipline through correct dress and enable them to become friends of students from other nations. Such a preparation is essential in the global village of the 21st century. The proof of our success is that prestigious international companies like Louis Vuitton, Ritz-Carlton hotels, Four Seasons, Starwood hotels and resorts, Claridges, Connaught and Beau-Rivage, among others seek out our graduates every graduation."

Francis was given a wonderful surprise for his 80th birthday. He was invited by the family to dinner and then taken into a room where an artist stood with a huge canvas. It was upside down and the artist spent 15 min splashing on paint. When he turned it right side up, there was a good likeness of Francis: a portrait in white on a black background by the painter Bouroullec.

LOCAL BOY MAKES GOOD

Erwin Mathieu is the typical story of the local boy who makes good. He was born in the small village of Agarn, Valais, which does not see the sun for almost three months of the year. He now lives in Crans-Montana which is one of sunniest parts of Switzerland. Erwin's father, Cäsar was a shift worker in the aluminum factory and money was short and life was hard. When the circus Knie came to Brig, they could only afford one ticket. His father went and on his return told the family what he had seen. Now Rolf Knie from the circus family is one of Erwin's best friends.

Like all the children in the canton of Valais, he spent six months of the year at school and the rest of the time, looking after the cows in the alpage called Unnär Aschp Weidu. At 16, he got a job at the Grand Hotel du Golf & Palace in Crans-Montana where he worked as bellboy. (See separate entry). He was a tall, handsome lad and as one of his main tasks was to open car doors, he was often tipped well by the hotel clients.

"One of the proudest moments of my life," he said, "was when I handed over a 1,000 Swiss franc banknote to my father with the money I had saved from my work."

Erwin is a keen cyclist and traveled by bike to school in Gampel. Later, when he studied administration at the commercial school in Sion, he covered the distance of 60 km every day from Agarn to Sion and back on his bike. This was not only to save money but he was also in training as a competitive elite cyclist. Erwin is still involved in cycling and is a good friend of Fabian Cancellara, the famous Swiss professional cyclist, whose career he follows.

Christina Foyle

The next step was improving his languages. He first studied French at Estavayer-le-Lac and then he went to England for six months to take the Cambridge exam in English. To support himself while he studied, he worked at the famous Foyles bookshop. It was there that he saw Christina Foyle driving in her brand new 1965 Rolls Royce Silver Cloud III.

"I was so impressed with the car that I asked the chauffeur if I could sit inside," he said. "The smell of the leather was wonderful. He told me the coachwork was by Mulliner Park Ward. It was very

5

elegant."

Today, one of Erwin's proud possessions is a Silver Cloud III that he purchased in 1975. His daughter and nephew also share his passion for cars. He completed his apprenticeships by working in top companies like Lloyds of London before he established the International Summer Camp in Montana (ISCM) with his sister and brother-in-law, Rudy Studer. He never looked back after that. He is proud that he has 200 staff on his payroll and he feels responsibility for each one.

"I treat people as I would like them to treat me," he said. "It is a question of respecting others and not being afraid of hard work. I have been my own boss since the age of 22 and have always set an example to my staff through hard work. I'm the first in and the last out."

Although, he associates with famous and the wealthy who send their children to the ISCM, he has never forgotten his roots. Every five years he takes his male school friends on holiday. It is another Valaisan tradition in which you always have a close relationship with your Jahrgänger or contemporaries.

One thing in business which is an anathema to him is short-term gain. He is often disappointed when he sees family business' sold for the sole purpose of financial gain.

The dream
"My dream has always been to build up my business for my family and then work with them in the business," he said. "You

learn from having that responsibility. With money, it is easily spent."

Erwin still owns his childhood home and has since added land to this property. "The access to our house was through a neighbor's garden which was once blocked by a wood pile. I remember that on one occasion I had to crawl over the wood to reach our house. Later, I was very happy to be able to purchase that piece of land and have better access to the house."

Erwin Mathieu is a good role model for his staff and is supported by his wife Patricia, daughter Tania and nephew, Philippe Studer. His roots are strong and through hard work became a great success.

THE WAITING GAME
François Rielle is one of the movers and shakers in Crans-Montana. His dream as a young man was to become a lawyer but instead he ended up the head of a major property company, Solalp. His parents ran a restaurant in the centre of Montana and when his mother died, it was decided that the cleverest of the sons would have a professional education. As his younger brother, Jean-Charles, was the intelligent one in the family, François went out to work.

"One day in 1965 I met a builder who proposed that I sell apartments in his building on the Moubra lake," he said. "He offered to pay me a 5% commission on sales which amounted to around CHF 50,000. So I put the prospectuses of the apartments on the tables of the restaurant where I worked during my holiday and spent the summer selling them. I was 18 at the time and was excited when I took round my invoice to the builder's office in Montana. He went to the big safe and gave me an envelope. When I opened it, I found only CHF 10,000. 'But you promised me CHF 50,000,' I said. 'Yes,' he said with a smile. 'But we did not make a written agreement, it was only verbal.'"

François was angry with the builder but managed to turn his exasperation into positive action. Shortly afterwards, he rented two ski boxes which served as a small office for his property business. Then he designed a logo that incorporated a symbol of the sun with an outline of mountains and called it Solalp. He told his father he would give it a shot for two to three months. As he was a good salesman, people began to bring him properties to sell. Within five years, he started to build his own apartments which he would sell.

Lex Moos

In April 1, 1961, Lex Moos came into force to limit the acquisition of real estate by foreigners. Fear spread among the other estate agents in Crans-Montana but François Rielle was not concerned. He believed that whenever there was a restriction, there was also an opportunity. It was inevitable that prices would rise because there would be a scarcity.The first step he took was to increase the standard commission from 3% to 5%.

It was the same situation recently with Lex Weber. While others threw up their arms in despair, he welcomed the new restriction on second homes. He calculated that there would be a 10% increase in prices.

"I had been lucky," he said, "as I had received planning permission to build many new apartments shortly before the legislation was promulgated. My philosophy has always been, 'To wait and to have the power to wait. Then the years will work for you and better conditions will prevail in the future.'"

François who is a citizen of Grimisuat and Sion has lived most of his life in Crans-Montana. He has a good insight into the Valaisian character.

"They have strong characters, "he said, "but their mentality is not open enough to others and to life. In the canton of Valais, you are wedged between two mountain ranges which limits your view. If you move over the mountains you can see the horizon. But if you don't you'll never see the horizon and that's the fate of most Valaisians."

He has two daughters and a son, Philippe, and one day, the eldest daughter, Karine who was 12 at the time, came home from school in tears. She was upset because her friend who sat next to her in class had changed his place. When the teacher asked the boy why, he replied that Karine's father had not voted for his father in the local election.

François was livid when he heard this and decided to leave Montana. He did not want his children to be exposed to such small-mindedness. The same day he went to Geneva, bought a building and settled his children in a private school. He stayed in Geneva for ten years until the children had completed their education and then returned to Crans-Montana. He divorced his wife in April 1987 and married Aloysia Ghio-Airaldi who comes from Alassio, Italy, in 1998.

Besides his property business, François is also the owner of the historic Grand Hotel Golf & Palace. The internationally known hotel has shown hospitality to royalty as well as celebrities since it was established over a century ago. In 1992 Princess Marcella Borghese who was a guest at the hotel introduced François to the owner who wanted to sell. He bought the hotel which also had 42,000 square metres of land and on which he built two apartment blocks. He is proud of the hotel which has synergy with his disco Pacha and restaurants Memphis and Le Chalet. (See separate entries).

ARISTOCRATS IN SWITZERLAND?

Switzerland is a democratic country and they never had an aristocracy. However, when prominent families supplied mercenary soldiers to a foreign power like France then the commanders of the regiments who fought well would be ennobled. Such is the case of the de Courtens who came from Italy and made their fortune by charging tolls over the Simplon.

"My ancestors served King Louis the XV of France in the important battle of Fontenoy in 1745 which he won against the English, Dutch and Hanoverians," said Dr Christian de Courten. "During the 18th century we had some 2,000 soldiers

5

in the de Courten regiment. The Valais was a poor canton and in order to survive a law was passed to allow men to serve as mercenaries with a rigorous code of ethics in war. Even the French author Voltaire wrote about the Swiss in his poem on the battle of Fontenoy:

Peuple sage et fidèle, Heureux Helvétiens
Nos antiques Amis et nos Concitoyens
Votre marche assurée, égale, inébranla-
ble.. ("Wise and faithful, happy Swiss,
Our ancient friends and citizens,
Your confident, even and unwavering
walk...")

Later, when the regiments were disbanded at the French Revolution, another ancestor, Eugene Antoine de Courten, headed the Papal Swiss Guards in the 19th century.

Count Christian de Courten who lives in Crans-Montana followed his father, Dr Henri 'Toto' de Courten into the profession of medicine. His father was a lung specialist who graduated from Lausanne medical school and worked in Zurich and Davos before he became one of the first pulmonologists in the Valais to work in the numerous sanatoria in Montana.

Geography of the body
"I remember also as a boy joining my father in the radioscopy van when he went around the canton," he said, "to check on the incidence of lung disease by taking X-rays. In Leuk, the locals could not pronounce radioscopy so they called it geography of the body! Later, when tuberculosis was cured by the antibiotic streptomycin, he switched to tourism medicine. I would help with the plaster casts."

"I admired my father because first and foremost he was a humanitarian and generous. He was never in the profession to make money and as a result he ended up every year with gallons of wine and tons of cheese which he was given in lieu of cash. I am paid properly but my patients still feel the need to give me gifts of wine and cheese."

The de Courten family went through a transformation when his father married a blonde Dutch women who was not only a foreigner but a Protestant to boot. When Christian de Courten took a step further and married Béatrice Halpern who was a Jewess, his two maiden aunts then established a foundation and sent the family archives to the historical department of the canton in Sion to prevent them from being disseminated outside the country.

"I met Béatrice when I was sent to a private school, Ecole Nouvelle, in Lausanne at the age of 12," he said. "She came from an Orthodox Jewish family from Rumania who settled in Switzerland and Israel before World War II. We immediately connected because both our parents had chalets in Crans-Montana. Later we both studied at the university of Lausanne, she law and I medicine."

Hadassah hospital
Before Dr de Courten specialised in opthalmology, he won a grant to do research at John Hopkins hospital in Baltimore. But he decided to resign because it required experiments with monkeys. Instead he went to Jerusalem to work in the Hadassah hospital for a year in a university eye clinic. There he encountered a fantastic

multicultural experience. Now he practices both in Lausanne and in Crans-Montana where he mostly performs opthalmic laser surgery. He has two daughters, Alix and Frédérique, who followed their mother's example and became lawyers.

PUBLISH OR PERISH!

Pierre Ducrey is one of those rare academics you would expect to find as a fixture at an ancient university like Oxford or Cambridge by virtue of his background of Ancient History, Latin and Greek. A hugely entertaining figure to whom you would gravitate in the dining hall as you would never know where his conversation would veer next. His stay at the Institute for Advanced Study, Princeton where Einstein once resided; the rectorship of the University of Lausanne; his 43 years of archaeological research in Eretria in Euboea, Greece; the history and sociology of war in Ancient Greece; or amusing accounts of meetings as a member of the Académie des Inscriptions et Belles-Lettres de I'Institut de France, Paris or as treasurer over two decades of the International Association for Greek and Roman Epigraphy (AIEGL).

He grew up near the Moubra clinic in Montana where his father, Dr Eugene Ducrey was a surgeon and bone-tuberculosis specialist. His parents met in a fortunate stroke of serendipity. His mother Lily had a car accident when she had fallen under a bridge at Riddes, Valais and was treated by his father. There is no better bond between a couple than when one saves the life of another. The only faux pas Dr Ducrey made in his life as a Catholic was to marry his wife who was a Protestant.

The grandfather on the maternal side was the textile industrialist and banker, Henry Heer, while some of the ancestors on his father side were professional soldiers who like many Swiss fought for the kings or popes in Europe and sometimes were ennobled. (The Swiss cantons were poor and were obliged to supply troops to foreign powers from the 16th to 19th centuries). One of the great grand uncles of Pierre Ducrey was a colonel in the court of the Tsar, his great grandfather and another great grand uncle were officers of the King of Naples and the two Sicilies. His great grandfather married an Italian woman. One of his sons, August Ducrey, was a professor of dermatology at the University of Rome. The other son, François, became a doctor and settled in Sion where his father was born.

Pierre Ducrey spent the early part of his youth in Montana where his mother organised a cultural salon at their home in the grounds of the Moubra clinic. There he met the first of the two spiritual fathers, René Payot, who was chief editor of the "Journal de Genève" and during World War II through Swiss Radio, the voice of liberty that gave an objective analysis of the events. (See separate entry).

History of golf

Payot was also the president of the Golf Club Crans-sur-Sierre and it was at his urging that Pierre Ducrey took up golf at the age of 7. He fought his way on golf courses over the years, had a handicap of 3, made the Swiss National team and at one time was the 3rd best Swiss golfer.

This is another side of his personality which you will rarely find mentioned in his remarkable career. Except, of course, if you ponder over the title of Histoire du golf de Crans 1906-2006 in his oeuvre of books.

When it came to choosing a career, Pierre Ducrey mentions the discussion he had with the Belgian banker and intellectual, Louis Camus, who survived a concentration camp and was treated by his father. He had decided to study history but the question was contemporary or ancient. It was a turning point in his life. Camus' answer was that everyone in the post-war era was into the contemporary stuff so why not do ancient history.

His father had eventually to close the clinic after they discovered the joint action of Rimifon and an antibiotic which controlled the disease. It was then that his mother decided to give her two sons a Protestant schooling in Lausanne and left Crans-Montana. Pierre Ducrey studied Greek, Latin and Ancient History at the University of Lausanne. Then followed up with a masters degree, spent four years at the Sorbonne in Paris and earned his doctoral degree in Ancient History at the University of Lausanne.

From then on he surfed the big waves of academia and ended up as rector of the University of Lausanne and being the third Swiss foreign associate member of the Académie des Inscriptions et Belles-Lettres de l'Institut de France.

War, the dreadful boomerang - don't throw it.

His second spiritual father was Jean Rudolf von Salis, a brilliant intellectual and author of many books who was professor of history at ETH Zurich. Like René Payot, he was an uncensored broadcaster during World War II and was critical against the Nazis to the extent that he was asked to be removed from his post by the Germans. Later as part of his philosophy, von Salis coined the term, "War, the dreadful boomerang - don't throw it."

Pierre Ducrey had known von Salis since his early childhood through his mother. Very soon, he discovered the interest of listening to his analysis of historical facts, past and recent. It is from von Salis that he learnt to take the long view of events. Although of Grison origin and Swiss German education, von Salis was formed at the Sorbonne and published his doctoral thesis on Sismondi in French. His cross-cultural education made him an early "European."

When Pierre Ducrey is asked about his philosophy, he does not quote Heraclitus on flux and fire. His reply is simple. "If you want a career in academe, there is a single aim to pursue. Publish or perish."

CANON CAMERA

Hervé Deprez who was born in Crans-Montana is third generation to run the photography shops. The history of Hervé's forebears reads like a Hemingway novel. His grandfather, Jean Deprez, was a Belgian soldier in World War I who was gassed by the Germans. He came to Montana to recuperate at the Belgian hospital, Chateau de la Boissere. When he recovered, he liked the area so much that he wanted to live here. Then he met Jeanne Crettaz who ran the village school. They married and he opened a photographic shop after he studied photography at the Vevey School of Photography. He died young and left his wife to care for their two sons, Telesphore 'Teles' and Jean-Marie. She continued to run the shop in Montana.

Teles also studied photography in Vevey. He specialized in publicity photos such as hotel brochures unlike his father who took portraits, landscapes and life in Montana. In 1966, he was invited to Japan to attend a Canon camera promotion. While he was in Tokyo, he met Jacqueline Dronsart from the Paris office of Canon. They married and Hervé was one of their children. Both his parents worked in the business and later opened another shop in Crans where they also stocked electronic products like televisions.

"It was the period of heavy equipment," said Hervé who recalled days with his father. "A photographer needed lights, tripod and bulky cameras and a boy to carry all his stuff around. At the age of eight, I was the boy. It was exciting to go on the photo shoots at places like Zermatt." It was inevitable that he followed in his father's footsteps and he was the third Deprez to study photography at the Vevey school. He joined them in the business in 1992.

"My father never used a computer," he said. "He had a film with 36 pictures and you were forced to do good work. Now with digital photography, it's quicker but you can become lazy as you can get thousands of pictures. The advantage is when you are on a photo shoot with the Patrouille de glaciers and there are 4,000 runners. You could've never coped with films and their 36 exposures if you needed to cover the event."

The new Y generation are not interested in printing their photos in spite of the high quality of photos taken with iPhones and iPads. The exceptions are family celebrations like a birth, a communion and a marriage. When it comes to pictures, Hervé is into realism not art. He enjoys taking photos of the environment around Crans-Montana such as the sunset, the glacier and the moon.

He still is faithful to Canon and among his photographic equipment is an EOS 1D Mark 4 and various lenses from EF 14 mm, 100 mm Macro and 300 mm. He also has a collection of photographic equipment which includes an old fashioned big Sinar camera complete with a black curtain, a cine Super 8 camera and an old Hasselblad.

He is married to Delphine Favre who comes from Venthône, just below Crans-Montana. (See separate entry Cave d'Anchettes). They have three children, Laurine, Benjamin and Morgane. One wonders whether history will repeat itself and one will go to Vevey.

THE AMBASSADOR

François Barras who was born in Cher-

5

mignon, Crans is the eldest son of Gaston Barras. He visited New York in the 1970s as student and now he is back as the Swiss Ambassador, Consulate General.

"When I first came to New York," he said, "it was the centre of arts. I was lucky then as I was introduced around by the Polish-Amercian writer, Jerzy Kosinski. I had met him in Crans-Montana where he often

came to ski. Today, I am surprised by how patrician the city has become."

"My home town was a good preparation for life and and career as it influenced me through its openness," he said. "Geographically, it has a most spectacular view of the mountain ranges around and the Rhone valley below. It fact, it reminds me of a vista from the deck of a ship. I've visited

many resorts and very few have such openness, a vastness of scenery. Other Alpine resorts like Gstaad or Zermatt are enclosed by a huge mass of mountains which imposes on you and can induce a feeling of claustrophobia."

François Barras grew up in Crans which attracted many tourists because of its famous golf course, the luxury shopping centre and beautiful natural scenery. It had a tradition of tourism which began in the early 19th century.

British invention
"Swiss tourism is a British invention," he said, "and the Swiss have hospitality in their genes. I have always been surprised that the greatest lovers of Crans-Montana have been the foreigners. They have had a great attachment to Crans and understood it better than the locals. As a diplomat, I have been lucky to meet people in my various travels and postings such as Dubai, Lebanon and Saudi Arabia who have found Crans to be a special place."

When he was 11, the friendship he had with an Italian classmate was an eye-opener. The boy, Pierre Magistretti, was from Milan and his mother who was a doctor had come to the resort for her health. (See separate entry). During the three years they lived there he discovered classical music - the mother played the harpsichord, intellectual debates and Italian literature. But then curiosity was always François Barras' greatest strength. This interest in people and culture later influenced him to obtain a Masters degree in Anthropology after his Bachelor degree in Law.

He re-connects with Crans through hiking which is a favorite pastime besides reading and listening to classical music. The hike he enjoys is from Montana to Leukerbad which is reasonably flat. He is a member of the Ancienne Cible which dates back to 1798 when Chermignon fought against Napoleon. The wines he favors are the Petite Arvine, Fendant and Pinot Noir from Ancienne Cible winery with coats of arms of the various Chermignon families. Sometimes, he likes to take his children to square in Chermingnon and tell them how deeply rooted they are. And thanks to tourism they are in the middle of the world.

"The main challenge today for the people of Crans-Montana," he said, "is to give soul to the urban sprawl that now represents the resort." It is unbelievable that Crans-Montana with a population of around 10,000 commands such global interest.

COW GIRL

Doris Mudry who lives in Lens is a lovely, exuberant personality. She still continues the ancient tradition of transhumance and grazes her cows on the alpage de Montralèche. Her herd of 120 cows and the same number of calves consists of mixed breeds of Montbelliarde, Swiss Brown, Holstein and Simmental. But she is not a cowgirl, she a famous cheesemaker who sells her Alpine cheese in several outlets including the local shop in Lens and in Manor Sierre and Sion.

"It was hard to start," she said, "because there were no women cheesemakers. But I won through and my cheese has the AOC (appellation d'origine contrôlée) stamp of approval."

From June to September, she lives up in the Alps in a chalet. The regime is tough as she is up at 2 am to make cheese from the milk of the previous day. Her shift lasts until noon. During that time she has embraced the cheese twice. She leans over the huge vat and feels the raclette to determine whether it is ready to take out. It must not be too dry. After dinner she welcomes visitors. Then it is early to bed at 8 pm.

Two types of cheese are made: The small tomme - a low fat variety made from skim milk, which can be eaten after three weeks and the richer raclette which needs at least three months to mature. The taste is exceptional for an Alp cheese.

"What do you expect when a cheese is made with milk from Alpine meadows," said Doris, "with hundreds of beautiful flowers."

Visitors are welcome on site where cheese can be bought direct from the end of August. The cheesery can reached by car to Zeuzier dam and then a walk up to the alpage de Montralèche. The other alternatives are by footpaths from Bella Lui to the bisse du Rho.

Foreign friends

4-STAR SUPERIOR

Marc Lindner comes from a family of hoteliers who together with his four brothers run over 30 Lindner hotels in seven coun-

5

Doris Mudry

tries. He is the CEO for the Lindner Group Switzerland which is based in Crans-Montana. He is also in charge of special projects and about to embark on the most exciting and challenging project yet.

"Crans-Montana is gearing itself up to become an all year round resort," he said. "It is exciting as there will be new developments, for example, the opening of the Pierre Arnaud foundation with its art exhibitions in Lens. But we will be in the forefront with a hotel and spa complex designed by a star architect, Mario Botta. Our hotel will become a signature for Crans-Montana and change its face forever through unifying both parts."

"The concept of the Lindner hotels is innovative. Most of their hotels are categorised as four star superior hotels but they surprise their guests with an upgraded service similar to five-star. To become a five-star establishment you have to have perfection and employ a large number of staff as they do in Asia and the Middle East. This is not possible in Europe."

"Guests who stay in these luxurious places," he said, "and pay expensive rates expect the earth. There is the guest who demands scrambled egg at 4 am or expects you to have a Domaine Leflaive Grand Cru Montrachet from Beune costing CHF 5,000 in your cellar and there'll be hell to pay if it isn't. But our answer is to surprise the guest despite our four-star rating. If a guest from our Majorca hotel comes to stay here, he will be pampered with all the things he likes because we know him well."

The family hotel chain was started by his father, Otto Lindner, the top German architect who opened his first hotel in Dusseldorf in 1973. The chain has won several awards in the hotel industry. Another innovative aspect is that they have a very high ratio of women in the business.

Big egos

"Women are good at hospitality," said Marc, "and they do not have big egos like men. We also respect the staff and I usually address them formally as I've known them from childhood and they just call me Marc. And our family are the easiest clients in the hotel as we take whatever rooms are available. We never block the suites. I sometimes stay in the most inferior room."

Marc Lindner likes Crans-Montana in spite of his friends who chide him that there is little to do besides playing golf and skiing.

"I grew up there," he said, "and I appreciate the 200 days of sun, the healthy air and the fantastic views of the valley. And within two hours, I can be anywhere - the connections are very good."

Crans-Montana is unusual from other resorts as it respects the privacy of its visitors. They come on holiday and do not want to be disturbed. This is not the case with places like Gstaad where people go to be seen.

"The billionaires can walk around in shorts and the only men in dark suits are the bankers," said Marc."I once got into conversation with a man who said 'I do watches and I'm sure you've got one or two of mine in your wardrobe.' I had never heard of him and he turned out to be a famous watchmaker. He enjoyed telling the story of how he started in the business - something few people would ask him about."

ALL YOU NEED IS LOVE

Jean-Claude Biver is one of the pioneers

"It's only when everything goes badly that everyone is interested in something new," he said. It required courage to espouse the slogan, 'Since 1735 there has never been a quartz Blancpain watch and there never will be.'

It took ten years for the company to be launched successfully. But in making such a stand with mechanical watches he has

and great innovators of the Swiss watch industry.

In the hour of crisis, he and Nicolas Hayek senior came up with solutions. Hayek invented the quartz and Biver stood firm with tradition. He brought back Blancpain from extinction by going against the grain with an all-mechanical line when everybody else jumped into quartz.

gone down in the history of watchmaking as someone who singlehandedly saved the industry from the quartz movement.

At Swatch, he was asked by Nicolas Hayek senior to turn around Omega. "I repositioned the brand and brought back its luster," he said, "through marketing and product placement mainly through James Bond films and celebrity sponsorships by Cindy Crawford, Pierce Brosnan and Michael Schumacher."

Perfect timing

But his greatest contribution to the watch industry was still to come with the young brand Hublot. It was founded in 1980 by Carlo Croco and featured the first natural rubber strap in the history of watchmaking. Jean-Claude Biver, who was a member of the Swatch Group Directors' Committee, was searching for a new challenge at the same time when Hublot had lost its direction. It was perfect timing!

Biver joined the company in 2004 as CEO and Board member and what he did was to take the idea of fusion outside the envelope. "I married yesterday with tomorrow, the past with the future, tradition with the new," he said. "It was a marriage of gold and rubber. Then gold and ceramics, Kevlar, pink gold or tantalum and rubber - and ultimately the fusion of movements marrying Swiss traditions with 21st century art of watchmaking."

There is a natural tendency not to look beyond the commercial success which was incredible with the Big Bang and fivefold increases in sales. But one cannot get away from the fact that what Biver did with Hublot was revolutionary. He launched the mechanical watch like a satellite into an orbit of a new Swiss watchmaking era. The fusion of unusual materials and styles are endless and can go on ad infinitum.

It begs the question of how was he inspired. "My moment of inspiration came when I saw I.M. Pei's pyramid in the Louvre courtyard," he said. "Here was a perfect example of what I wanted to achieve with Hublot."

Biver was born in Luxembourg on September 20, 1949 and his family moved to Switzerland when he was ten. As a boy he was fascinated by a steam engine and watches - how energy generated could create movement. He was educated at St Prex school, Collège des Morges and the University of Lausanne and arrived in Le Brassus, a village in the Vallèe de Joux, Vaud with a HEC diploma.

It was the cradle of complicated watchmaking that would mark him for life. He settled near a farm which would later become Blancpain's head office. He started with the prestigious Audemars Piguet and was determined to learn all he could about watchmaking from the world's best company.

All through his life, he has been guided by the philosophy that has been epitomized by the Beatles song, 'all you need is love.' "If you love someone, you show them respect," he said. "The word love is synonymous with respect. I would not respect myself if I didn't behave with love towards my customers, my suppliers and competitors. I couldn't have an affair with another woman because it would demonstrate a lack of respect for my wife to whom I'd vowed to be faithful in marriage. Above all, it would show a lack of respect for myself which is an anathema."

Moubra lake

Jean-Claude Biver who lives on a farm in Tour de la Peilz has an apartment in

Crans-Montana near Moubra lake. He started skiing in Champery and followed his friends to Crans-Montana.

"It's not Zermatt, Verbier or St Moritz for skiing," he said. "It's a place where you can ski with your father, teenagers or your six year old. Verbier on the other hand is limited for multi-purpose skiing. Nowadays, I don't enjoy shooting down the slopes doing 3 km in 3 minutes. I prefer to ski halfway and at 11.30 to sit on a terrace in the sun and enjoy raclette and a Fendant. You can do that in Crans-Montana when you start early. The slopes are in sun and not in the shadow and you avoid crowds which I hate when I ski."

Cindy Crawford

He was at the helm of Omega when the company took over the title sponsor from Canon of the European Masters Tournament. "Up to then the event was regional and had no important golfers or celebrities participating," he said."We put it on the map because we brought along top personalities and did a lot of PR. I had Cindy Crawford to open the first Omega European Masters Tournament and also invited Ivanna Trump. My brother Marc who headed IMG did his best to promote the event with sportsmen and entertainers who were under contract with the company.

"In the end it was a win-win situation because it was a genius of an idea. It helped to reposition Omega as a top luxury brand and highlighted the Crans-sur-Sierre as the most beautiful mountain golf course in the world."

Besides his business which he looks upon

as a hobby, he is also a cheesemaker. His cows spend the summer in the alpage where they graze on Alpine meadows full of flowers. The special taste is imparted to the milk and cheese. He produces around five tons, all of which is consumed by family, friends and specific restaurants where he donates the cheese. He refuses payment as he wants to be in total control of the distribution. "I want to be master of my cheese until the last piece," he said.

Who knows, Biver might also be thinking of another marriage of rennet from the milk and rubber?

AUDITIONING FOR A MOVIE

Liz Bestenheider who lives in Lens originally grew up in California. She is a qualified skiing instructor for children and a hiking guide for summer and winter with snowshoes and ski touring. Liz is the ideal outdoorsy person as her parents were hippies and big on hiking and camping.

"Of course, I also surfed in California and was once asked by a casting director to audition for a movie," she said with a smile which highlights her good looks. "It was for a movie with Richard Gere who starred with two women. But I was not that keen on acting."

She met her husband, Thierry, in Los Angeles and they decided to come back to Crans-Montana and raise a family. As a foreigner it was quite tough because she did not speak French and people in the village tended to have a parochial attitude towards outsiders.

"I liked a challenge and when my children were at school," she said, " I would see other mothers with children in the street and invite them home to have a pie. At first there were no takers, but one day a woman agreed and that broke the ice. Other mothers followed and I was soon integrated in village life."

The beautiful surroundings in Crans-Montana are ideal for outdoor activities which she takes advantage of with her children. "I pick up them up after school," she said, "and we go off somewhere on a walk, snowshoeing or skiing." In this way she got to know the picnic spots, the outdoor cafes (buvettes), the lakes, the rivers, the glaciers, the mountain paths without any names and the bisses or irrigation canals.

Consequently, as a hiking guide she can offer a variety of outdoor activities. There are the easy, the medium and the difficult hikes. However, it is important for her to know the physical status of her clients as well as their preferences. Sometimes her clients do not know what they are looking for.

Her favorite trail is the Montana to Leukerbad. There is a diversity of scenery and one lands up in a thermal bath and having soup before you return by bus. But the most spectacular route is along the bisse de Roh. However, it is limited to hikers who do not suffer from vertigo. Sometimes, people become slightly dizzy en route and she ropes them for security. There is another easy to middle trail along the Plaine Morte glacier and around Mt Bonvin where the scenery is also spectacular.

Liz Bestenheider

LONG ROAD TO CHETZERON

Sami Lamaa comes from a family of hoteliers and restaurateurs. One grandfather Leopold de Sepibus worked for César Ritz in London and Paris and another ran a hotel in Beirut. He himself was born and lived in his parents' restaurant in Montana. When the Chetzeron cable station was closed in a restructuring programme, he spotted an opportunity. He would open a new kind of restaurant on the slopes at 2,112 m. There had been complaints of the food of the mountain restaurants over several years.

But the decision to convert Chetzeron into a hotel was not the easy part. It took 13 years to realize his dream! But what an adventure it was for Sami to achieve his aim.

The long delay was due to many factors. "First, I had to face my own conflict," he said. "Should the building be a wooden chalet which was the opinion of most people or of stone? It took me some time to make the decision. I investigated and found that other buildings on the top of passes like the Grand St Bernard and the Simplon were of stone. So I decided on stone."

There were times when he wanted to give up but a visionary in the shape of a man appeared who provided solace and friendship. Louis Begault was the one and later became a partner and friend. Another stroke of luck was finding the right architect. (See separate entry Perils of relocation). Most of them were developers under the skin. Ambroise Bonvin from Actes Collectifs proved right for the project and even put in extra time at no cost to ensure a successful outcome.

"I put the years of waiting to good use," said Sami. "Napa, my Thai wife and I, traveled to see examples of another mountain hotels and restaurants. We also explored the concept of Alpine food by visiting Swiss, French and Italian resorts. I spent time on details like special stitching on the curtains and finding the right baskets for baby potatoes."

The Chetzeron restaurant was opened in 2009 and was a success from the first day. The sleek stone finish with the modern glass window frames and the spacious terrace with the planking stained with extra virgin olive oil captured the hearts of the locals and visitors alike. The view

too from the terrace was an outstanding feature. The cuisine was a surprise too for although it was good food, it was at moderate prices and the presentation was superb.

Overnight he had become a restaurateur par excellence. Then he began the next stage as hotelier and four rooms were opened in Chetzeron and a further 12 are planned to open in 2014.

"My concept with the Chetzeron was based on three elements," said Sami. "Silence - you don't have the noise of a cableway station. Spaciousness - I've often seen so much crowding at mountain restaurants and I deliberately put more space between the tables so people didn't feel squeezed in. Finally, Swiss quality of the food and of the furniture."

Since Chetzeron opened, the quality of the food on the slopes has improved. More work is being carried out on the hotel as it includes a swimming pool and a special terrace for the hotel guests. One thing is certain - it will not involve a long delay.

THE MOUNTAIN VILLAGE MADE ME

Professor and Director Pierre Magistretti is a neuroscientist at the École polytechnique fédérale de Lausanne (EPFL) and has made significant contributions in the field of brain energy metabolism. With over 100 articles published in peer-reviewed journals, he likens his research work as delving into the unknown.

But he is no stranger to being placed in

unknown situations. As a 11 year old boy he was taken from the bosom of the family in Milan - where uncles, aunts and cousins all lived together in the same building and dumped in the mountain village of Crans-Montana. His parents who were both medics and had separated, decided that he and his younger brother, Philippe, should be sent away.

His mother who needed a period of convalescent accompanied them. They arrived on September 19, 1963 and his mother rented an apartment from Mrs Odette Barras who together with her husband Gaston ran an estate agency. (See separate entry). It was a huge challenge for a city boy to settle in a Valaisian village where he knew no one.

He was first placed in the primary school because although he spoke French, his writing skills in the language were poor. After couple of months, the teachers moved him into the secondary school. As he had missed the first lessons, he was introduced to an intelligent boy, François Barras so that he could copy his notes. (See separate entry).

"We became fast friends because we both were top in the class," he said, "and younger and smaller than the other pupils. I was bullied by the big mountain boys - once I was thrown into a small ravine and broke my leg but got my own back because my weapon was that I was clever in class."

"François spent a lot of time with us as he enjoyed the intellectual company of my mother. He also learnt about classical music as she played the harpsichord. His parents, Gaston and Odette did not have enough time for their children as they were quite busy with the property boom in Crans-Montana."

Pierre's mother left after three months and the boys were put into a boarding school which they never attended because their father insisted on a public school education. Pierre skied and was an ace at golf. "The Severianos Ballesteros golf course is not a major golfing challenge," he said. "It's easy and the balls go further because of the altitude but the scenery is breathtaking."

Soon he was invited to join the Swiss National Golf team for juniors and later played in the Swiss National Golf team. His handicap was one.

"What I learnt through my Crans-Montana experience," he said, "was that you had to survive or die. I had integrated and later was respected by the other mountain boys. When I returned to Italy after my education, I decided to become a doctor. But at the time, Italian universities were in the middle of political turmoil so I decided to enroll in a Swiss university. In order to do so I needed a Swiss high school degree (Maturité) so I returned to Crans-Montana, studied alone for a year and passed the exam successfully which would enable me to do medicine in Switzerland. It was tough as I totally alone and boarded with Angèle Rey at Les Gentianes who became like a mother to me."

5

Youngest professor

He never looked back after obtaining his medical degree at Geneva University and his PhD at the University of California, San Diego. He became at 35, the youngest professor to occupy a chair at a Swiss medical school. Before his current position, he contributed to interdisciplinary studies by making a link between biology and the subconscious. His research together with the psychiatrist François Ansermet revealed that experiences, emotions and memories all leave their mark on the brain by modifying it and thus making each person unique.

Crans-Montana played a significant role in his life and he became a Swiss citizen in 1974. He still maintains an apartment in the resort.

"It's certainly a melting pot and a good school for life," he said. "Other school chums have also done well. François Barras is a Swiss ambassador and Vincent Barras is a Professor at the University of Lausanne. Perhaps, it has to do with the invigorating air and broad horizons. More seriously, in Crans one has the possibility to meet successful and interesting people from all over the world and that is certainly a stimulating environment for a young brain."

CHARITY GALA

Linda Barras is the president of the charity La Nuit des Neiges. It was started by her brother-in-law François Barras, the Swiss ambassador in New York, over 30 years ago and is the highlight of the social calendar in Crans-Montana.

The charity gala which is held in February each year usually donates funds raised to local and international causes. Among the recent beneficiaries have been Sport for life and Cerebral Valais. Sport for Life is a playful initiation into a sport for young children and some 1,500 have benefited through the programme. Cerebral Valais is a charity run by the canton for children who suffer from cerebral palsy. La Nuit des Neiges will support in-home services as well as contribute to holidays abroad for their families which is outside the remit of the cantonal charity.

Linda who is Armenian by birth met her husband, Christian Barras at one of the galas. (See separate entry) So the charity is close to her heart.

"I enjoy living in Crans-Montana because it is multi-cultural, sunny and dynamic," she said. "There is a good selection of shops such as Hermes, Chopard, Louis Vuitton and Julia & Co for clothes. The resort is also near Martigny as I like to visit exhibitions at Pierre Giannada Foundation. But sometimes I miss having the opera, museums and the theatre nearby which I had when I lived for many years in Geneva."

SERBIAN SUCCESS

Alexandar "Aco" Kalajdzic who is the son of a farmer, was born in a small village outside Belgrade, Serbia. He went to school in Trieste and to earn pocket money, he worked in pizzerias and Italian restaurants.

When he came to Switzerland, he served

an apprenticeship for three years at the Belmont hotel in Crans-Montana. (See separate entry). He also learnt to play golf there as the hotel is next to the first tee of the Jack Nicklaus 9-hole course.

His first job was as a chef at the Boulangerie-Restaurant Gerber and then as head chef at the Les Violettes restaurant before he was promoted to manager. In 1998, he had the opportunity of establishing his first restaurant, Michelangelo. It was a stressful and exhilarating experience as he and his wife, Joka, slept on the premises until the opening.

With the restaurant, he had two number 1 objectives. To serve the best quality food and give the best service. He specializes in fresh homemade pasta and wood-fired pizzas.

Although he had no top chefs as mentors, a compliment enough is that the famous British chef, Michel Roux senior, eats at Michelangelo.

"It's not difficult to trace my inspiration," he said. "Look no further than my mother. She always used fresh food to cook our meals. My parents are now in their 80s and when I return home, I look forward to her roasted chicken and dessert of cream cheese rolled in crepe and cooked in the oven."

Aco has been a Swiss citizen for over 15 years and also has the restaurant Oliveto which his wife, Joka, runs. His son, wants to study at the Les Roches campus in Shanghai. (See separate entry.) The name Michelangelo has nothing to do with the famous Italian artist. His friend Angelo found him the location for the restaurant and he in turn had promised him to name the restaurant after him. But Angelo did not mean much on its own so Aco added Michel and Michelangelo was created.

5

Chapter 6. Wine and Cheese

Wine

The canton of Valais is the famous wine growing district in Switzerland. Vines are grown along a 50 mile strip of the Rhone valley, mainly on the sunny, steep slopes of the south facing Bernese Alps which extends from Martigny to Brig. It is a glacial valley with a relatively flat floor and some vineyards are on slopes as steep as 70°. The construction and maintenance of these are labour intensive and costly. Much wine here is grown at high altitudes from around 2132 ft to 3772 ft at Visperterminen in the Upper Valais, which is one of the highest in Europe.

The Valais climate is favourable to viniculture as it is very dry because the surrounding mountains prevent access to rain bearing winds. Summers are hot, winters and early spring cold, though tempered by the warm dry föhn blowing up from the Mediterranean.

A wide range of grape varieties is grown in the Valais, reflecting the varied terrain, the historical isolation, the rich viticultural past and the vibrant wine growing culture today. The valley is characterized by the presence of 59 grape varieties with 26 red and 33 white. It is recommended to try the native varieties which are unique to the Valais. The whites include Petite Arvine, Amigne, Humagne Blanche while the reds comprise Cornalin and Humagne Rouge.

In Crans-Montana, the winemakers are found below the Haut Plateau in Flanthey which is an old terrain for wine. The majority are only in the first or second generation of independent production as large cooperatives were responsible for winemaking in the past. Each winemaker produces a wide range of good wines and one is spoilt for choice. However, I have selected several exemplars. The best way is to discover them is to ring up the winemakers and try the wine in their carnozet, a special room for wine tasting. Do not forget to ask for the snack of cheese and dried meat - the Walliser teller that usually accompanies it.

Tough guy of wine

Cave la Romaine
route de Granges 124,
Flanthey.
027 458 46 22
079 214 08 77
info@cavelaromaine.ch

6

Joël Briguet is the tough guy of wine who has a great zest for viticulture. From the age of seven when he worked with the family in the vineyards and helped his father who was a vine nurseryman, he always knew that he wanted to be a wine grower. From then on nothing could stop

him. First a diploma in oenology from Changins, then at 22 bottling his first vintage and at 26, he established a new cellar. In 2010, at the age of 46 he cut the ribbon at his new premises at Flanthey. A modern winery with a elegantly curved wine storage cellar, a carnozet or wine tasting area and a stunning panoramic view.

His vineyards which comprise 12 hectares

are between Sierre and Sion. The grapes are from vines over fifty years old and undergo pre-fermentation cold maceration before yeast is added.

Joël concentrates on high quality and low yields per hectare. It has paid dividends for the top of his range, the Empereurs label, has earned many distinctions. Both of his whites Petite Arvine and Heida, took a silver at the prominent Vinalies Internationales competition in Paris. The Heida which is usually grown at high altitudes has taken well to lower slopes of Flanthey. The reds too have done well at competitions. The Pinot Noir Castel d'Uvrier won a gold at the Mondial Pinot Noir; the Cornalin Coteaux de Sierre a couple of gold medals; and the Humagne Rouge Coteaux de Sierre several gold medals. The latter is an impressive Humagne by its concentration and ripe fruit and is a wine of freshness and finesse.

Joël barrels along motivated by his passion for wine. He shows his earthy character when questioned about his wines. "There is no secret about good wine," he said bluntly. "The wine is made in the vineyard. In the cellar, we work to preserve the fruit."

He has an energetic team to support him. Vincent Tenud is cellar master and his wife Edith is in charge of the administration and sales.

Altitude and wine

Bagnoud Wine
Chemin du plat de Valençon 15
Flanthey

027458 6055
info@bagnoudvins.ch
www.bagnoudvins.ch

Nicolas Bagnoud who lives in the hamlet of Valençon, Flanthey, has a purpose-built winery. He cultivates six hectares and has a remarkable knowledge of the terroirs, the microclimate and the individual characteristics of the grape varieties. He has a rule of thumb calculation of altitude and weeks of growth. Every 100 m of altitude you ascend slows the maturity of the grapes by about a week.

"For example, a white grape like Humagne Blanche or Petite Arvine," he said, "needs more heat and sun and is grown in the valley at 100 m. The red Cornalin which is an indigenous grape and difficult to grow, requires shallow, dry earth. But it also demands best sites exposed to the sun and is late to mature. Chardonnay, on the contrary needs more time to mature and is put on the higher slope.

The range of red wines include the slow grower, Pinot Noir, of which the barrique version is spicy with smoky overtones and Parchets de Valençon that won a silver medal at the Mondial du Pinot Noir. Nicolas also produces some splendid blends like the white Cuvée Or Fin from Chardonnay, Pinot Blanc and Païen and is matured in wood. His sweet wines such as the Hermitage and Pinot Clairs - a late harvested blend of Pinot Gris and Pinot Blanc, are special.

6

Noble country
Cave d'Anchettes
Les Bondes 3
3973 Venthône
027 455 1457
076 4301457
anchettes@bluewin.ch

If you want to see the most impressive winery building, then cross the border from Crans-Montana into the Noble country of Venthône. The building that houses Cave d'Anchettes was designed by the late Simon Favre-Berclaz who had outstanding artistic talent but was not a qualified architect. It is a fitting memorial to the winery he founded in 1969.

Jérôme, the son, and his mother Fabienne run the vineyard which covers 10 hectares and has 30 grape varieties. They range from the traditional Fendant and Pinot Noir to some which are quite unfamiliar in the Valais like Viognier from France and Pinotage from South Africa.

"Our philosophy is to do a lot in the vineyard," said Jérôme, "and as little as possible in the cellar."

The focus begins with planting quality vines as his mother, Fabienne, is a vine nurserywoman who trained at Changins. The selection of the right vine stock can make a difference to the life of a plant which can last for 30 years or only six or seven years. Another aspect of her work is to detect disease in the vineyard. For example, red blotches on the leaves are a sign of a virus.

Little is left to chance as they institute soil and leaf management, strict yield control and ripeness checks. The philosophy continues with the vinification which is very natural without added yeast, sugar and enzymes. A minimum of sulphites are used for preservation and not to stop fermentation.

"If you close your eyes and imagine you're walking through a wood," said Jérôme, "you can see wild strawberries when you taste our Pinot Noir. It has fermented twice in a barrique for 18 months. A two year old raclette cheese compliments the wine. It is a complex marriage with vanilla and smoked almond."

Jérôme is also an enthusiast of sweet wines which are made from late harvest wines often picked in January. Of particular interest is the blend called Yacca produced from several red varieties and aged for 18 months in a barrique.

Winemakers
A selection of winemakers in Flanthey.

Gaston and Eric Bonvin
Route de Lens 40
3978 Flanthey
079 4542533 /079 6376158
eric@cavebonvin.ch
www.cavebonvin.ch

Oaked Pinot Noir and Pinot Noir from raisined grapes.

6

Vins Bruchez
Sébastien Rey
Route de Granges 91
3978 Flanthey
027 4581214
www.vinsbruchez.ch

Fourth generation winery specializes in Dole, Dole Blanche, Pinot Noir and Fendant.

Cave Cordonier et Lamon
Arthur Cordonier
Chemin du Tsaretton 50
3978 Flanthey
027 4581257
vins@cordonier-lamon.ch

Extensive wine list of 29 wines.

Domaine Montzuettes
Charles-André Lamon
Rue St Clement 8,
3978 Flanthey
0792207580
ch.-andre@montzuettes.ch
www.montzuettes.ch

Ex-vine nurseryman who specializes in the temperamental Cornalin.

Cave Nouveau St-Clement C.Lamont & Cie
Clément and Christian Lamont
Rout de Condémines 20
3978 Flanthey
027 458 4858/ 079 4491464
clamon@cavelamon.ch

Wines vinified separately to preserve individual characteristics.

Cheese

Alpine cheeses originate in the remote valleys of the Alps, isolated from one another by lush mountain meadows. The low salt content of Alpine cheeses is one of the things that give these cheeses their sweet, nutty taste and elastic, meltable texture ideal for raclette.

The mountain meadows, filled with a wonderful array of wildflowers and grasses, also play a key part in the complex flavours of these cheeses. Cheese makers spend several months up in the alpage to make their tomme and raclette. If you want to meet one like Doris Mudry, then drive up to Zeuzier dam and walk up to the alpage de Montralèche. The other options are by footpaths from Bella Lui to the bisse du Rho. (See separate entry for Doris Mudry).

Ferme des Trontières
Samuel Berclaz
Pafouer 48
Randogne
027 481 8891
0774449070
email: sberclaz@vtxnet.ch

You can buy direct from the cheesemaker whose cows graze on the Alpine meadows. Samuel Berclaz is the second generation to be involved in the company which was started by his father, Jean-Claude over 40 years ago.

His father began as a cowherd at the age of ten when he lived the whole summer up in the alpage of Prabaron in a small mayens

looking after some seven cows.
Three sorts of cheeses are sold and include a small, round low fat cheese called tomme (a month old), the large raclette (three months old) and the year old cheese with a strong flavour. Petite Arvine goes well with cheeses except for the old cheese which should be drunk with a red wine.

Laiterie Au Petit Chalet
Ave. de la Gare 4
Montana
027 481 2246
florian.bonvin@bluewin.ch
www.laiterieaupetitchalet.ch

The dairy stocks homemade fondue or 'moitié-moitié', Alpine cheeses, mountain honey, homemade jam, meringues and Gruyère cream.

Chapter 7. Camp and Schools

There are additional benefits in coming to Crans-Montana for both parents and children. If parents have children aged 8 to 17, they might like to enrol them in the famous summer camp in Montana where they will have a super time. There are three sessions which each last three weeks from the end of June until the end of September. The parents will be free to participate in a host of activities including golf, hiking, shopping and wine tasting, among others. In the end, both parties will be satisfied.

The other option is for young adults to enrol in the Les Roches, the international school of hotel management located in the village of Bluche. The courses which include practical as well as theoretical subjects are fun and prepare students for a global career - a necessity these days. It also helps them embrace and respect other cultures, differences and behaviours. A measure of its success is that prestigious brands outside the hotel industry like Bloomberg and Louis Vuitton are keen to employ their graduates.

There is an educational opportunity for adults too. They can learn languages through social activities rather than with headphones and repitition of the words. Académie de français in Crans has an innovative course which takes its students away from the classroom.

International Summer Camp Montana
Route de la Moubra 43
Montana
027 486 86 86
Info@campmontana.ch
www.campmontana.ch

My father was a visionary

There are summer camps and summer camps. Some offer serious sports training in tennis and swimming but another model uses European traditions in the development of physical and intellectual achievement for boys and girls aged 8 to 17 years. The International Summer Camp Montana (ISCM) which has been run by a family of Swiss professionals for over 50 years, offers a wide range of activities which enriches campers in mind, body and spirit.

Philippe Studer and his cousin, Tania Mathieu are owners and directors of the camp. Tania's father Erwin is in charge of the administration and her mother, Patricia is camp mother. (See separate entries.)

"Our principle element at the camp," said Philippe Studer, "is for children to have time to dream. In the three weeks they are with us, they learn to be independent, to get on with others and to grow as a person."

The fact that they have a high loyalty of between 70%-80% - the return rate is three to four times, is proof of its success. It is also not uncommon to see the second generation of campers and even some of the third generation. Erwin Mathieu who has seen some 48 summer seasons, can identify children whose grandparents were there.

As ISCM is truly international - there are children from 58 different countries, each camper has the opportunity to broaden their outlook by meeting people from different countries and varied backgrounds. The camp is multicultural and not religious. The children are divided into four age categories and then into groups of eight. The boys and girls are kept separate except for evening activities and river rafting. There are counselors and sports instructors at the ratio of 1 to every 2 campers. The campers follow a proper programme over three weeks.

Sports, languages and fun

"It's a mixture of sports, languages and having fun," said Philippe. "The school programmes are strict as they consist of lessons in the morning and sports in the afternoons."

Philippe oversees the programme while

Tania Mathieu

Philippe Studer

Tania who is an accomplished rider is responsible for sports and events. Both Philippe and Tania grew up in houses in the camp grounds. He was educated at the Lausanne Hotel School of Hospitality and she at the Glion School of Hospitality. The idea of the international camp came from Philippe's father, Rudy, who had worked during the summer at camps in Arosa while he studied economics at Basel University. He liked what he saw but he knew that he could improve on the idea.

"My father was a visionary with a flair for business," said Philippe. "He liked sports, children and riding. He met my mother, Erica, and her brother, Erwin at a horse jumping competition which he won. Soon after, my father invited my mother to visit him at one of his camps. She came from a

small village, Agarn, in the Valais and was scared when as a 20 year old she encountered all the children around."

"Later, my father arranged a meeting with both my mother and my uncle in Visp. His proposal was to establish a summer camp in Crans-Montana which was booming at the time. They would buy an old clinic which had enough accommodation for a couple of hundred children. He would be in charge of the programme, my mother would be the camp mother and my uncle the administrator. That is how the summer camp started in 1969."

Erwin Mahtieu

Camp mother

Erwin Mathieu, Pat Mathieu

Pat Mathieu never had fixed roots until she
came to Crans-Montana at the age of 22.
She had led an itinerant life until then. Her
father who was a diplomat and later a busi-
nessman, traveled around with his family.
She even visited Crans-Montana before as
a 2-year old. But it had been an unsettling
experience as she remembered that she
had been evacuated from the Forest hotel
before it burnt down. (Now the site of
Supercrans tower).

During the youthful years of travel, she
was fortunate as she had language skills
and could adapt to the environment around
her. She speaks English, French, German
and Spanish fluently.

"I'm what you call a member of the global

village," said Pat. "And if you move around a lot, I've found that it is important to have a knowledge of languages in life. I'm easy going with meeting strangers as I like talking. At the camp where we have children from 58 countries, I can put my communication skills into action."

She met her husband Erwin in 1974 when she worked as a secretary at the five-star hotel Royal. She had seen a lot of him as they lived in the same building, the Residence Crans Leman. When they met she was astonished to find that he was the owner of the building as well as one of the partners in the ISCM. After the marriage, she led an independent life and for 10 years ran the Chanel boutique in Crans.

"I'm completely into clothes," said Pat. "I've always known exactly what I wanted to wear. If I wore fuchsia for example, my complete outfit would be in the colour and even my accessories and underwear. But in the evening I always wear black and white."

There is little doubt that she is one of the most glamorous camp mothers in the world.

Les Roches International School of Hotel Management

Bluche,
Randogne
Crans Montana
027 485 96 00
info@lesroches.edu
www.lesroches.edu

Ticket to global careers

The most exciting presence in Bluche, a village in the Randogne commune, is the campus of Les Roches. (See separate entry on Francis Clivaz). During the semesters, the student body is like a mini United Nations as 98% of them are international. The breakdown of the students varies from Asia (37%), Europe (35%), Americas (16%) and the Middle East (12%). Les Roches also has other branch campuses in China (Shanghai), Spain (Marbella) and Jordan (Amman).

When you enter the building between classes, the vast reception area is filled with a diversity of cultures. And they all speak English with rich variety of exotic accents. But there is more than meets the eye. The French student, Richard Mahe from Paris found that 'Les Roches is not just a school, it's a way of life.'

He immediately felt at home on the first day he arrived. To start there was strong sense of belonging to a community and the uniform they all wore brought the students together. Another aspect was the interaction with the teachers in the classroom. They were always available for a chat and also around at weekends as they lived on the campus.

"This was so different from university," he said, "where you sat in a classroom and took notes and rarely had contact with teachers. At Les Roches, you also got into a routine quickly. Lunch at the restaurant, evening meal at your residence where all rooms had fridges and weekends you ate out. Some students even go as far as

Geneva."

"I studied law at Rennes university and then decided to change my career to hospitality," he said. "It was risky and I didn't know whether it would work out or not."

Richard who has just finished his postgraduate degree at Les Roches is excited as he has landed his first job in London. He was snapped up by the ultra-luxury hotel group Rosewood and will start in July, a month after he has graduated.

Chou Yun - you can call me Roger, comes from Xi'an in China and will leave Les Roches with a Post Graduate Diploma (PGDII). He has just accepted a job in the management programme at the Mandarin Oriental in Shanghai. He had other offers from the Kempinski and the Ritz Carlton which he turned down. They wanted him to do an internship before he joined them.

"I majored in English language and literature in Beijing," he said, "and one of my teachers told me about Les Roches. I have traveled in Italy-Rome and France-Paris and found them very splendid. I didn't experience any culture shock. I found the people friendly and as I've visited Shanghai which is an international city, I'm used to multiculturalism."

Internationalist

Sonia Tatar who is the CEO Les Roches worldwide all campuses is the ideal choice. She is a true internationalist who speaks English, Arabic, French and Italian and also has lived in many countries like Tunisia, France, Italy, Belgium,

USA, Caribbean before Switzerland. Her business experience is a perfect match for Les Roches as it includes cruise ships, Euro-Disney and INSEAD - the renowned business school in France.

When her predecessor, Arie Van der Spek, Senior Vice-President of Laureate Hospitality Education worldwide, handed over the reins to her, he gave her a model of Michelangelo's staircase from the Laurentian library, Florence. It was fitting as she had also gained a diplôme d'études approfondies (DEA) for studies on Michelangelo.

"This staircase if placed on your desk will remind you every day about this challenge," he said, "of taking Les Roches to further heights." Under his watch the students grew from 600 to 1,200 a semester.

"What attracted me to Les Roches is the opportunity to combine the hospitality and service sector with education," she said. "There is also the opportunity to share my experience and expertise with the next generation, the leaders of tomorrow. Contributing to the education and success of young graduates within such a dynamic, growing and exciting sector is very fulfilling. We prepare students for an international career and to have a global, and open-minded spirit. We help them embrace and respect other cultures, differences and behaviours. We make them strive for high standards - excellence in the *savoir faire and savoir etre*."

The curriculum is geared to give a sound academic grounding through an Anglo-American approach. "We use external examiners from British and Irish Universities," said Jeremy Hutchinson, director of Academic Affairs, "and then in the final semester round off their specialism with a range of general education subjects in addition to the core curriculum. So we turn out students who are not only good at hotel management but can converse with clients in a cultivated way."

Académie de français
Rue du Pas-de-l'Ours 6,
Crans
027 480 4938
info@swissfrenchacademy.com
www.swissfrenchacademy.com

Académie de français is an innovative language school where students do not wear headphones or 'repeat after me.' It is geared to teaching adults French, English, Italian, German, Spanish and Russian in combination with sporting and cultural activities. It sounds too good to be true but the classroom has one of the longest cherrywood bars in the resort. It fact, it resembles an English club.

"It's frustrating to learn languages when you're an adult," said Neva Hay, the director, "but it's so easy as a child. Therefore, I set up a novel programme which enables our clients to use their experiences to master a new language on all fronts. The results are startling with a 100% pass rate, and most of her students achieve 80% and above in the official French DELF examination which is equivalent to the Cambridge English language certificates. The best way to teach adults is to create a convivial atmosphere for learning." Unlike other language schools, the classrooms also extend outdoors into the beautiful landscape of Crans-Montana. You have options to combine learning French with cultural activities, golf, skiing, hiking, wellness and business. For the programme to be effective, the minimum period is two weeks.

Alongside the bar are the classrooms which are fitted with state-of-the-art teaching aids. "The interactive multi-touch white board enhances the retention powers for both the auditory and visual learner," she said. "It captures the students' attention with a wealth of material which can be instantly incorporated into the lessons.

Neva Hay hails from Melbourne, Australia and now lives with her Swiss husband in Crans-Montana. A sparkling personality with a shower of ideas, Neva Hay came up with the original concept of the Académie de français.

Chapter 8. Cafes and Restaurants

There are three kings of cuisine in Crans-Montana. Franck Reynard at the Pas de l'Ours, Pierre Crépaud at the Mont Blanc and Laurent Morard at the Monument in Lens. Tips: If you eat at Mont Blanc ask for a table in the kitchen. By the way, Franck Reynard also has a place on the slopes called Les Violettes.

CAFES

Cafe-Bar 1900
Rue du Pas de l'ours 2
Crans
027 480 19 00
info@campmontana.ch

It is cool. Open 24/7 during season and serves the last meal at 11.30 pm.

The coffee is tops as it is French than rather Swiss and you get a petit four with it. They serve a bistro menu without any frills. Sandwiches are unique as you have a wide choice of all ingredients from a list on a card. Specialities also include pancakes and panini.

The situation is convenient as it is just round the corner from Rue du Prado which has the best luxury shops in the alps. Brands like Vuitton, Gucci, Hermès, Chopard as well Hublot, Rolex among others. (See separate section Shopping).

Taillens
Boulangerie-Pâtisserie /Tearoom
Sylvie Taillens
Rue du Grand-Place 7
Crans
027 485 40 80
www.boulangerietaillens.ch

Boulangerie-Pâtisserie/Tearoom
Nicolas Taillens
Ave. de la Gare 8
Montana
027 485 40 80
nicolas@boulangerietaillens.ch
www.boulangerietaillens.ch

Boulangerie-Pâtisserie
Magasin Violettes
Montana
027 485 40 62

Rue Théodore Stéfani
les Acacias,
Montana
027 480 36 80

Route Principale 26
Lens
027 483 25 34

8

Taillens is an institution in Crans-Montana and very much like the Soda Fountain of Fortnum and Mason in London. There are two tearooms, one in Crans and the other in Montana which are open all the year round. It is the place to be seen and a good place to to observe the locals and tourists over a coffee or a glass of wine. If you come regularly the friendly staff, some of whom have been there for 30 years, will even anticipate your order. Some visitors to the resort have been coming to the bakery for over 40 years. They are usually greeted by Reto Taillens who has retired but appears in the Montana tearoom. The establishment is now run by the third gen-eration, Nicolas and Sylvie Taillens.

After her schooling, Sylvie was sent to Cologne in Germany to learn German and then to Bournemouth to learn English. She passed the commercial diploma for operating cafes before joining Taillens. Sylvie's responsibility is the tearoom in Crans which she opened with her mother Marie-Claire in 1991.

"It's my life," she said, "and I spend more time here than at home." She and her brother Nicolas who is in charge of the production grew up with the sweet aroma of the dozens of breads baked each day and surrounded by all the glorious patisse-rie. Black Forest cake is her favorite.

De rigueur in the tearooms is to select and pay for your patisserie before you sit down. If you are peckish you can choose from the snacks in the menu or in Sylvie's tearoom, they can make you a special club sandwich or an omelette of your choice.

To delight the locals, Nicolas not only has a bread of the week but also launched the innovative summer and winter collections of patisserie. One winter he created double mousses with raspberry and calamansi flavors as well as banana and peanuts. The tearoom is always full of surprises and one can also discover their variation of the moreish lemon curd.

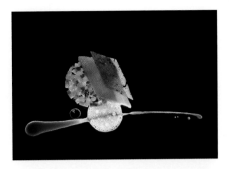

For the third generation of Taillens women, life in the patriarchal society has changed.

"I can now go on holiday on my own with girlfriends," she said, "whereas my mother's generation would never do that. The other difference is that the boys and men in Crans and Montana no longer came to fisticuffs over women or as a sport. We could meet the opposite sex socially at discos and nightclubs like Pascha. But the social life in the resort can be improved. We definitely need facilities like a swimming pool with a fitness and wellbeing centre which can be a focus for families."

Sylvie has two children and it is likely that a fourth generation to run the business is in the offing.

There are two restaurants at the hotel, the gastronomic L'Ours and the bistrot des Ours. Both are under Franck Reynaud. He has a Michelin star and a high Gault Millau rating. The interior of the restaurants have a cosy ambiance due to the extensive use of both old and modern wood decor. The Bistrot des Ours gives pride of place to local flavours, while in the gourmet restaurant you can savour a selection of extraordinary culinary combinations.

"My philosophy is to bring emotion through the food," he said. "I go directly to the essentials. For example, in a rabbit dish, I stick the kidneys on top of a square terrine and for balance I add an upright morel with a garlic flower."

Franck dreams of dishes and then has to

RESTAURANTS

Hostellerie Pas de l'Ours
41 Rue pas du Pas de l'Ours
Crans
027 485 9333
contact@pasdelours
www.pasdelours.ch

equate the dream with reality. His cuisine consists of art pieces which stir the emotions. The shapes and the colours are far beyond what one would anticipate on a plate of food.

"I see the dishes and the flavours in my head and I need to experiment to realize them. I don't have any mentors but I'm influenced by good chefs."

Le Mont Blanc restaurant (Le Crans hotel & Spa)

Chemin du Mont-blanc
1 Plans Mayens
Crans
027 486 60 60
info@lecrans.com
www.lecrans.com

When you eat here your palate will be titillated with a cornucopia of tastes, flavours, aromas and combinations from a gourmand menu. Pierre Crépaud is a chef who is a creative improviser and has been given his head at Le Mont Blanc. Already he is high up on the Gault Millau chart and it is question of time before he enters the Michelin lists.

"My soul is is written on the pages of the menu," he said. "Take the starter with foie gras. I have added medjoul dates, crispy spicy ginger toast and jelly of mulled wine. Other dishes with unusual combinations like crispy cappuccino of Jerusalem artichokes served with smoked butter and accompanied by the heart of veal filet. Or scallops and roast pumpkin, bread sections with truffles and beef marrow and steeped in Humagne wine. But each dish is offered

in a responsible-eco-rational spirit. Some of the produce is from Fair Trade and the seafood on offer is based on preserving marine biodiversity."

Pierre who is sportive and likes skiing and hiking to recharge his batteries is a nature lover. He enjoys roaming the countryside in search of wild blueberries, mushrooms and chestnuts and uses flowers in his cooking like the blue flower borage which has an iodine taste and is served with fish.

The best introduction to his cuisine which is contemporary even avant-garde and rooted in tradition is to try his set menus. Le Grand Huit or roller-coaster which assails your taste buds with wildness and unpredictability. The 55, a lunch menu which costs 55 CHF, is composed of five courses including the dessert and served in 55 minutes.

If you really want a total novelty, you can eat at Pierre's table in the kitchen where the staff serve you between their work. The table is big enough for eight people but you have to reserve.

Le Monument Bistrot Gourmand

Route d'Icogne 3
Lens
027 483 19 82
www.lmbg.ch
lemonumentlens@gmail.com

Lens which has the grandest church in Crans-Montana, the amazing Christ the King statue and the two ancient bisses, now has another prestigious addition, the Monument.

Laurent, Marie-Anne Morard

This is the bistrot Gourmand which is presided over by the young king of semi gastronomic cuisine, Laurent Morard. He is a talented, self-taught chef who developed his taste buds from childhood. He learnt from his mother's kitchen through tasting all the dishes she cooked. For the rest, he served his apprenticeship as a chef and learnt from traveling around the world.

"I start with the visual impact of a dish," he said. "It has to surprise the diner. Then it's the taste. It has to be clear-cut and not smothered under sauces."

One dish which is a knockout is the Moussaka d'agneau confit. It's round and looks ike a hamburger but then it has a lamb chop on top. Underneath is macerated aubergine on mashed potato and then a

8

ragout of lamb. The cardamon flavour is interwoven - a wonderful green cardamon from Guatamala that imparts a freshness with a citronella aroma.

"When I was in Marrakesh, I was dazzled by the spice market," said Laurent. "It made me aware of the role of spices and how they helped not only digestion but defined taste."

Ideas for his innovative cuisine are mainly mental. "Laurent does not spend hours with experimental dishes," said Marie-Anne Morard, his wife, "It crystallises in his mind and then it's right the first time."

The wine list is comprehensive and contains some gems. Monument which is located between the commune and the church, is in the old manor and is some 15 minutes from Crans-Montana.

Le Michelangelo
Avenue de la Gare 25
Montana
027 481 09 19
079 214 01 31
www.lemichelangelo.ch
pizzeriamichelangelo@bluewin.ch

Oliveto restaurant and bar
Place du Marché
Montana
027 480 2222
www.lemichelangelo.ch
pizzeriamichelangelo@bluewin.ch

Both restaurants serve fresh homemade pasta and have a good range of Italian food. This includes wood-fired pizzas, pastas from penne to spaghetti and lasagne; meat from osso buco to escalopes and steak; fish from prawns to tuna and sole. The desserts include the special baba au rhum ou limoncello, glace vanille crème chantilly. They are both run by Aco Kalajdziczic. (See separate entry).

La Diligence
Hotel and restaurant.
Route de la Combaz 56
Montana
027485 9985
info@ladiligence.ch
www.ladiligence.ch

The top Lebanese restaurant in the Valais has a varied menu and several specialities including Couscous Royal and meat cooked on the table-top grill - the Tatar hat. It is part of a charming chalet style hotel owned by the Lamaa-de Sépibus family. The rooms are quiet with good views of the Alps and the Rhone Valley and have television and free WIFI access.

One of the main reasons for their success is a warm welcome which is given to everyone who crosses the threshold.

"What I learnt from my dramatic studies is to adapt to the part you play," said Françoise who is the second generation to run the establishment. "In the restaurant it's the same because each person is different and you have to adapt to their personality. To communicate in the right way is challenging because at the same time you mustn't lose your own personality. A neighbour might pop in to drink a beer or the Princess from Monaco come to have a meal. I treat them all the same irrespective of social class or age because I enjoy the human contact."

Françoise is also the sommelier and has an innovative approach. She asks the guest, "Where would you like to travel? To Lebanon or to the Valais." Once the destination is established she finds out the wines they normally drink. It is only then that she will recommend a wine that suits the food. The restaurant has an excellent wine list to which new wines are added each year after wine tastings.

"Wine is all about emotion," she said. "It's like art. We learn from others but trust only in ourselves."

Françoise Lamaa grew up in Bluche. As a child, she led the typical sporty life of skiing and snowboarding in winter and hiking and skateboarding in the summer. She was fortunate because some of her friends were older and helped her to perfect her technique. Soon Françoise and her brother, Sami, became the village champions of skateboarding.

"We were free for most of the time," she said, "as our parents were busy running the restaurant and we never had a private life. There were always other people around like the guests or the staff."

Françoise had a penchant for the theatre and at the age of 14 decided that she would become an actress. After matriculation, she went to study acting and dance at the conservatoire of Geneva and Lausanne.

She acted in the whole gamut of plays from Greek drama to Moliere. Once when she returned to Bluche for a few months holiday her parents received a proposal about a restaurant.

"They had managed restaurants in the past," said Françoise, "and now there was an opportunity to buy La Diligence in Montana. It was an exciting moment but it needed four people to operate. It was a restaurant and an auberge with eight rooms. So Sami who was working in Zurich and I returned to work with them."

It was a challenge as her father, Farhan Lamaa, had only cooked Lebanese food for friends before. Now the idea was to put it on the menu at 1,500 m. The Lebanese cuisine was an immediate triumph as Crans-Montana is a cosmopolitan resort. After almost two and a half decades, it has become top Lebanese restaurant in the Valais and also attracts local people from Sierre, Sion as well as Martigny.

Boulangerie-Restaurant Gerber

Route du Rawyl 35
Montana
027 481 62 47
www.brasseriegerber.ch
info@brasseriegerber.ch

A boulangerie and restaurant which is open at 6 am for breakfast. It is known for its pizzas and is popular in winter after skiing or ice skating which is across the road from Gerber.

Chermignon cafe, restaurant and B&B

route de Tsanveulle 18,
Chermignon d'en haut

027 483 2596
info@auxbonsmatinsdecapella.ch
www.cafechermignon.ch

This is the village restaurant with a difference. It is a bistronome where one can be surprised by the cuisine and with la carte menus fit for a gourmand.

The interior wood panelling with black and white portraits of the Duc family strikes the right ambiance of comfort and tradition. A sign hung on the wall completes the impression for it says: 'Enjoy the little things in life...For one day you will realize that they were the big things.'

"When people come here whether they are locals or visitors," said David Duc, the third generation of owners, "we want them to enjoy themselves. They can kick off their shoes and stay until closing time. I can say in French - Le Plaisir de faire plaisir or in English - Your pleasure is our pleasure."

There is only place for 30 people and when it is full it is full. There is only one meal session and the menu offers seasonal and regional products. Cote de boeuf is popular as well as fish dishes. Both David and his wife Elizabeth supervise the menus.

David is proud to continue the tradition of his grandfather and father who not only ran the bank across the road but operated a cafe for the benefit of the locals. They could keep an eye on the place from their office to see who went in and out and sometimes pop over to join their friends

for an apero. The customers paid for the wine and helped themselves to a snack of cheese or dried meat in the kitchen.

Elizabeth has complemented the restaurant by offering a B & B. So if customers have lingered long enough over their splendid meal in the evening, they can also stay the night. She graduated in fine art and has displayed her artistic talent in the decoration of two luxury rooms.

Memphis restaurant
Rue du Prado 19
Crans
027 480 44 20
info@lememphs.ch
www.lememphis.ch

A lounge bar and restaurant. It is a place to see and to be seen in Crans.

Le Chalet
Rue du Prado 5
Crans
027 481 05 05
info@lechaletcransmontana.ch
www.lechaletcransmontana.ch

The restaurant is in a distinctive wooden chalet. It offers different fondues, raclette cooked over the fire, grilled meats and 'spit roast' specialities, farm chicken, beef ribs and leg of lamb.
Tips: Go for après-ski at Zerodix (027 481 0090, www.zerodix.ch), which has an outside bar next to the Crans gondola. Skiers congregate on tables set out under large red awnings.

8

Edo Restaurant Japonais

Rue Cantonal Sierre-Montana 43
Bluche
027 481 70 00
reservations@edo-tokyo.ch
www.edo-tokyo.ch

There are Japanese restaurants and Japanese restaurants but you have to come to Bluche to find the most remarkable of its kind. Here the ancient traditions of food in Japan are passed on with enthusiasm and emotion. As is to be expected the quality is premium as well as the authenticity because all the basic materials such as sauces and sake - there are four types, are imported from Japan. The chefs are Japanese and have their own personal sets of knives which they sharpen every day until the utensil is totally diminished.

The restaurant is a little window of Japanese cuisine and offers a selection of food unlike the eateries in Japan where each one is specialized. For example, you will find a place that only serves grilled eels. Most people would at best have heard of sushi which must be eaten with rice at room temperature otherwise the steamed rice loses its taste and texture. It is a dish which was originally eaten in the street whereas sashimi which has no rice is favoured by the upper classes in Japan.

"The restaurant has evolved over the period of ten years," said Phillip Zhan, the owner. "When I first opened the locals were under the misunderstanding that Japanese food consisted only of raw fish. It is like the Chinese misunderstanding that the Swiss only eat chocolate. So it was im-portant to provide information on the food which the staff are now trained to do."

"From the start, I set a high standard through top quality food and authentic materials," he continued, "so that if a Japanese ate anything here his palate would immediately recognize that the taste was genuine."

What is most extraordinary is that the man behind such an establishment is Chinese and from Beijing. He married a Japanese women, Kaori Arai, whose family had been in the restaurant business from the Edo period - 17th/19th century. Both of them studied hospitality and hotel management at Les Roches a couple of streets away and they stayed ever since. (See separate entry). When they graduated they worked at Les Roches for several years and later decided to open their own restaurant. The opportunity came when Phillip bought the schools' tennis court and first built his home and then the restaurant.

"It's important to understand the cultural difference between the Japanese way of eating and the European way," said Phillip. "The Japanese tend to wolf down their food and then move on to another place where they can socialise over drinks or tea. Whereas the Europeans like to socialize over their meals."

Edo has the typical ambiance of a Japanese restaurant with black square tables and a terrace with a great view of the Alps. Pride of place is given to two artefacts which usually contain saki. There is Oke, a huge white cask with a capacity of 72 litres which is opened with mallets during a Shinto festival, weddings and other celebrations and a smaller lacquered bottle called Taru.

Below the restaurant is a Chinese take-away, Atlas Panda, which Phillip has nicknamed Riceland. It serves a selection of common dishes with rice and is moderately priced. A catering service is also available.

What Phillip will come up with next is anyone's guess. But with his dedication and sincere personality, he has made an outstanding contribution to the gastronomy and social life in Crans-Montana. Edo is well worth a visit and a reservation is recommended.

On The Slopes

Chetzeron Mountain restaurant and hotel
027 485 08 08
076 576 4176
mail@chetzeron.ch
www.chetzeron.ch

Chetzeron is a big cable-car station that was converted into the resort's trendiest mountain restaurant. It is cool with a stone, steel, glass and wood building and a huge indoor dining room with tables which are wide apart and can seat 60. The terrace outside has double the capacity with 120 seats and luxurious sunloungers.

During the skiing season, piping hot stews are served in special soapstone pots which retain the heat. A particular favourite is bio lamb stew covered with vegetables

and polenta. In summer, barbecues are popular and include the much favoured homemade sausages. There is a choice of lighter meals like salads or soups. Typical Valaisan specialities are also be on the menu as well Alpine cuisine like gnocchi with à la fondue.

Enjoy amazing views and a well-deserved rest in quiet surroundings. Some might find it hard to leave and Sami Lamaa the owner has added four hotel rooms to accommodate such discerning people. More are planned in the future.

In the summer, it is the jumping-off point of the black trail for the bikers who reach Crans in 4 - 5 minutes. In winter, for the red ski-run Chetzeron.

A special treat for hotel guests in winter is to ride the snow cat up or down to Chetzeron. It takes 14 passengers and is an exhilarating experience. The restaurant can be reached via ski or snowboard from the blue piste at Cry d'Er or alternatively you can walk from the pedestrian track at Cry d'er or Merbe in 20 minutes.

Cabane des Violettes
www.cabanedesviolettes.ch
info@cabanedesviolettes.ch
027 481 33 95/39 19

At an altitude of 2,200 m Violettes is located at the top of the gondola of the same name. Franck Reynard is the chef and it offers soup, salads, pasta, gnocchi, polenta and Valaisan specialities. (See separate entry). It has a new terrace below the restaurant.

8

Chapter 9. Property Services

The chapter consists of architects, real estate agents and a cautionary tale of relocation.

Gabriel SA
Architecture Studio
Immobilier Clair-Lac B
Rue Centrale 3
Crans
027 481 4410
www. gabrielsa.ch

Gabriel SA is a member of Comina Architecture which has offices in Sion, Verbier and Crans-Montana. It is a one-stop shop because it also has a qualified real estate agent on the premises.

Architects

Grégoire Comina is the second generation of qualified architects. His father René Comina established his first practice in Sion in 1947. The Crans-Montana office which was opened in 1985 covers domestic, commercial and industrial buildings. The Ecole des Pilotes in Sion, the five-star Le Crans hotel in Crans-Montana and the four-star La Cordée des Alpes in Verbier are examples of buildings designed and built by the firm.

"Our bywords are creativity, care of detail and thoroughness of architectural concept," said Comina. "But we also deliver a project on time and at the quoted price."

De rigueur is to interview the client about their requirements. Next to show them examples of chalets or commercial buildings. But if it also includes the purchase of land, it is important to go with the client to the site and gauge its suitability for building. The trend today is to use old wood or a mixture of new and old wood in most buildings.

"As architects, we have good contact with the commune's planning department," said Comina. "We are knowledgeable about the regulations of heating systems, electricity and the individual requirements of each of the six communes in Crans-Montana." (See separate entry).

If it is a new building, then inspections have to be carried out by the relevant commune and the canton to see whether everything has been carried out according to the law. Only then can the householders move in.

9

Real Estate

Ludivine Comina who lives in Crans-Montana is the daughter of Grégoire. She is one of the few real estate agents who has a federal license to practice.

"It means that I have a lot of technical knowledge as well as I know about Swiss law pertaining to property," she said. "I can answer most of the legal questions and construction questions. With my clients, we usually go direct to a notary. We are also up-to-date on Lex Weber and on the camera drone which enables clients to see the views from the all floors before the building is built."

Agence Immobilière Barras
La Residence,
Rue Centrale

Crans
027 481 2702
info@agencebarras.ch
www.agencebarras

The agency which was the first to be established in 1954 is run by the pioneer of real estate, Gaston Barras and his son, Christian. (See separate entries).

Services included construction, sale and rental of apartments and cottages, administration, management and AXA Winterthur Insurance.

SIC Société immobilière de Courtage
Agency Crans
Rue Centrale 21
Crans

Régine Reynard

027 480 3727
info@siccrans.ch

Agency Montana
Rte Louis Antille 1
Montana
027 480 4450
info@siccrans.ch

An agency founded in Crans-Montana in
1999, they focus on sales as well as rental.
They also manage and maintain property.
Régine Reynard, a former head teacher,
runs the company.

Agence Solalp SA
Route du Rawyl 21
Montana
027 481 56 56
info@solalp.ch
www.solalp.ch

Established over 45 years ago, the agency
sells apartments and chalets. It also offers
numerous apartments and chalets to rent
on a weekly, monthly or annual basis. It
also has a property management section.
(See separate entry François Rielle)

Holiday Services
Route Barzettes 4
Montana
027 480 4122
0794583867
info@holidayservices.ch
www.holidayservices.ch

Gaby Piazza offers a unique service to
apartment owners. She is a girl Friday
and undertakes all sorts of services for
owners. From property management which
includes checking the post and arranging
the bills to be paid, organising rentals to
preparing the apartment ready for occupa-
tion on their arrival which includes food
in the refrigerator, clean linen and general
cleaning.

A charming couple, David and Sheila
Sellar from Sussex, UK had been looking
to buy a property abroad for some time.
They met through a colleague and had
dinner with Gabi the night they arrived
in Crans-Montana. Then she organised
viewings of apartments over the next six
months. One apartment in Les Barzettes
turned out to be the one they bought.

"I knew it was for us from the moment
I walked in," said David. "We bought it
in 2006 and Gabi was wonderful. She
handled everything for us which was
marvelous as she speaks a fluid technical
French which we lack."

"Little things are not too much for her
to do," said Sheila. "Once before our
departure, the light in the bathroom broke.
We mentioned this to Gabi as our daughter
was due to arrive soon after. It was fixed
without any problem. Now our daughter
has also bought an apartment from her."

Another owner from the UK, commented
on her services. "She takes out the hassle
of owning an apartment. We spend about
six weeks a year in our apartment and
she manages everything in-between from
rentals to the accounts."

Gaby has a background in real estate and
worked for a local company for 22 years

9

Eddy van der Vliet

before she set-up Holiday Services. She buys and sells properties for clients who invariably become friends. Renovations are also part of her portfolio and she can advise on contracts as well as property taxes.

Elite Immobillier

Grand Place Ouest
CP 129
Crans
027 480 4440
079 220 3722
info@montana-immobilier.ch
website.montana-immobilier.ch

Elite real estate agency undertakes to buy, sell or renovate property in Crans-Montana. It is run by Eddy van der Vliet who has good local connections with banks, ar-

chitects, decorators and craftsmen. He can obtain authorizations for Swiss nationals to buy an apartment or chalet as well as for foreigners who require residency in order to buy properties in Switzerland.

There are over 40 real estate agents and Eddy van der Vliet has a small and elegant office. As he wants to put the client immediately at ease, they step inside in what looks like a living room. Although, he was born in Amsterdam, he has lived in Crans-Montana since 1981.

He married a local girl Marlène Praplan from Icogne commune and is an avid supporter of the resort. (See separate entry). He founded the classical music association, Les Sommets du Classique and is a member of the Crans-sur-Sierre Golf Club as well as their 1,000 club.

"My philosophy is carpe diem," he said. "I can enjoy every day because I live in such beautiful surroundings. When I wake up in the morning and see the panoramic view of the mountains, it makes me dream."

JP Emery Architectures
Residence les hauts du Golf
Route des Mélèzes 22,
Crans
027 4819641
079220 40 37
jpemery-sa@netplus.ch

Jean-Pierre Emery who was born in Crans-Montana was educated as a town planner in Paris. He lived in Le Corbusier's Swiss Pavilion while he studied at the International City University. When he established his practice in the resort, he built big chalets such as Sapins d'Or, Manga and Les Perles.

"I've no favorites because I'm a good father." He laughed. "I like them all."

The demand has always been for vernacular architecture because people who come from the cities want typical Swiss chalets and not modern homes.

"The result is that the chalets which are built tend to be a mixture of Grison, Savoy and Bernese styles," he said. "The resort is popular because it is within easy reach of Paris, Zurich and Milan and has a healthy climate."

The trend today among his clients is to have huge chalets covering 500 - 1,000 square metres to accommodate extended families.

"But the first requirement is have the best chalet in Crans-Montana," he said with a smile. "That's easy if you start with the best architect." He laughed.

"These huge chalets are unusual as they need to have a ludique ambience," he said. "If you are to lodge grandparents, parents and grandchildren under the same roof then you have to amuse them. So you have a swimming pool and jacuzzi at the top of the list, followed by fitness, sauna, home cinema, carnozet, billiard room and even a cabana at the swimming pool."

Besides chalets, he landed two plum commissions. There is the prestigious art centre, the Pierre Arnaud foundation which is a modern ecological building in Lens and a large hotel and spa complex in Crans-Montana. (See separate entry).

9

Relocation

Perils of relocation
Angela and her family came to live in Crans-Montana eleven years ago. They bought land in one of the communes and wanted to build their dream house. Each country has its oddities when it comes to relocating and Switzerland is no exception.

"We had planned that it would take a year to build," said Angela, "so we rented an apartment for the duration. But it took two years. It was ridiculous! We ended up living with the builders."

"The first lesson was about buying the land. It was not straight forward. When you enquired about the price the seller answered, 'what are your prepared to pay?' If your offer was too low, they were not interested. It was a game of poker.'"

The biggest surprise was to find that objections to planning proposals was a sport. Neighbors can oppose plans for no reason and put a stop on the building for several years. They will withdraw their objections if you pay them off.

"We bought an extra parcel of land next door for an extension," she said, "and later found that we could use little of the land for actual construction because of the proximity to Swiss Confederal forest which we also own. It meant that we couldn't build within 10 metres of it. But we could chop down all the trees within that area. If anyone denounced us we had pay a fine CHF 500."

The next lesson was the short working hours of the builders. They appeared at 8 am, had a coffee break at 9.30, stopped for lunch at 12.00, had a tea break 3 pm and left at 4 pm. Nice work if you can get it!

"During the supervision of the work, I was constantly reminded that it was a patriarchal society," she said. "Sometimes, the builders looked at the plans and said,'It's better this way.' My retort was 'It's my choice, it's my house.' Little respect is given to a woman giving instructions."

Later they had another surprise about architects. Some are qualified and others who are not, can still call themselves architects. They found to their peril that they had hired an unqualified one.

"There were three choices of wood for construction," said Angela, "and we chose fir because it could be stained. It had been written down in the contract which had been accepted by all parties. But we found that pine had been used. Instead of solving this through litigation - you can't win in Swiss courts, we each paid a third of the costs to get the right wood. This is despite the fact that one of the parties was 100% at fault."

There was a major problem which loomed and threatened the health of the family. During the construction, concrete which was used for the walls was held in place by shuttering that was pinned by plugs. When the plugs were removed the builders had forgotten to fill the holes. So Angela had to nurse a baby with mushrooms growing on some walls.

"We had holey walls that looked like Emmentaler cheese," she said.

When the house was finally built, they could not have a fence as the snow destroyed all fences. The situation allowed neighbors and others to roam freely on their property. One day, Angela and her family came home to find people picnicking and enjoying the view from their garden. When the intruders were told that they were in someone's property, they replied, 'no harm's done' and left.

"Sometimes we would return home and

see the neighbors' children using the swings and slides," she said. "They didn't seem to have any understanding of privacy. It was the same with deliverymen or chimney sweeps. They would just turn up when it suited them in spite of giving us a specific time."

"Another surprise was to discover that the high proportion of costs of a house," she said, "goes into the plumbing and electrical installations because of Swiss regulations which create a cartel."

The key to reducing the pitfalls of building a house or chalet is to find a qualified architect. They will also have contacts at the commune for planning and can ensure that oversights like the failure of installing soundproofing will not happen.

"There are very strict government regulations on seismic and heating loss reduction which increases building costs dramatically," she said, "but no regulations on soundproofing. We have an inbuilt 'unofficial telephone system' through the water pipes as insufficient soundproofing was used. But can you imagine if you lived in an apartment block where there no insulation. It would be pure hell!"

9

Chapter 10. Hotels

The strength of Crans-Montana has always been the hotels. The first was the hotel du Parc which was built in 1893 when the journey up from Sierre by mule took four hours.

"What built the resort was the hotels," said Joseph Bonvin, owner of the Art de Vivre, "whose owners funded the first Tourist office. But since then there was a trend for hotels to be converted into apartments, a course which was unthinkable for me. It is like the story of owning a cow. It gives you milk. But if you sell the cow, there is no income from the milk."

The resort is well placed for accommodation with a wide range of hotels from luxury, first class, comfort, economy, totaling together some 50, to apartments and chalets, B & B, mountain huts, group accommodation and camping. A selection of establishments have been made below:

Hotel Belmont

Rue du Belmont 4
Crans
027 485 01 01
email: hotelbelmont@bluewin.ch
www.hotelbelmontcrans.ch

The 3-star hotel has a beautiful situation alongside the Jack Nicklaus golf course with its trimmed greens in summer and on the doorstep for cross-country ski pistes in winter.

All the balconies are south-facing and the views of the alps are spectacular. The Belmont offers its guests a peaceful and restful stay. You're just a few steps away from sport facilities and the centre of the resort.

The hotel is run by the second generation, Alain Duc, who has an apartment on the premises. It is highly recommended by golfers. Green cards for the Crans-sur Sierre Golf Club can be purchased at a special discount.

Hotel du lac

Promenade de Grenon 1
Montana
027 481 34 14
hotel-du-lac@bluewin.ch
www.hoteldulac-crans-montana.ch

Quiet and central situation by Grenon lake which is a few minutes on foot from the ski lifts and from the centre of Montana or Crans. The three-star family hotel is run

10

by the third generation, Yves Klingler.

It has a splendid view of the Valaisian Alps with a small garden and a large car park. An innovation is the local beer, La Marmotte, whch is brewed in the hotel.

Auberge Lago Lodge

Lac Grenon
Montana
027 480 2037
auberge-lagolodge.ch

The budget price guesthouse is near the Grenon lake and offers rooms that accommodate up to eight people. Doubles and family rooms are also catered for.

Grand Hotel du Golf & Palace

Allée Elysée Bonvin 7

Crans
+4127 485 42 42
info@ghgp.ch
www.ghgp.ch

Claudio Casanova is a hotelier extraordinaire who not only runs the Grand Hotel Golf & Palace but is the president of the board of the Les Roches, the international school of hotel management in Bluche.

"Today, the grand hotel presents a challenge," he said. "Like the Gstaad and St-Moritz Palace hotels it has adapted to social changes and to the emergence to a new clientele. The volumes have to be used differently. We offer all the modern facilities like spa, beauty and fitness centers. There is also a medical centre with a doctor on the premises. We

From l. to r. Claudio Casanova, Greg Norman

are no longer open all year round and are closed in May and November. This gives us distance and a chance to think of new niche markets."

As a result of a customer survey, a new food and beverage concept was introduced. They employed several chefs to cater for different cultures. For example, the Chinese prefer to eat their own cuisine and an Asian chef prepares a menu for them. The same applies to Jewish or Muslim guests who have special Lebanese chef to cook their traditional dishes.

Essentially, it is a hotel beloved by golfers and the official hotel for the Omega European Masters Tournament. It is situated near hole-16 and next to the tee off for hole-17. Most of the top players like Greg

Norman and Ernie Els have stayed there. "I studied at the Lausanne School of Hospitality where I met my wife Annie who was also a student," he said. "One of my first jobs was at the Dorchester hotel in London. I enjoyed my time there and as I lived in Queensway, Bayswater, I had a short walk through Hyde Park to the hotel. When I returned to Crans-Montana, Annie and I ran several hotels as directors."

"In 1978, we became independent and had our own hotel the Colorado. Our break came in 1983 when we bought the Beauregard hotel. Then in 1998 we renovated the hotel with a new identity. Instead of giving the walls a coat of paint and hanging up reproductions, we hit upon the idea to have bedrooms decorated by artists. Each room was different and a work of art. It was fun

10

and we could do anything because it was our own baby."

In 2004, Claudio joined François Rielle in managing the Grand Hotel Golf & Palace. It was on the historic site where once stood the wooden hut which served as cloakroom, bar and restaurant for Sir Henry Lunn's golf course. Later the hotel du Golf et des Sports was built which was extended to become the current Grand Hotel du Golf and Palace. It followed in the traditions of the other great hotels famous for their glitz and glamour, exquisite luxury, first class service and limitless indulgence which attracted royal families and celebrities.

"Our USP is most usual," he said with a laugh. "We do not have air conditioning. You just open the windows and breathe in the remarkable mountain air which is the healthiest in Switzerland. The views too from the balconies offer breathtaking views of the Alps."

Hotel Guarda Golf
Route des Zirès 14
Crans
027 486 20 00
info@hotelguardagolf.com
www.hotelguardagolf.com

Everything about the 5-star hotel has been hand-picked. The superb location is close to the shopping centre in Crans and has a view to the fairway. Even the name which in Romansch language Guarda means Look - Look golf.

From the moment you arrive, you cosseted in a friendly ambiance. The doorman wel-

comes you and takes the car keys as there is valet parking. The luggage is taken to your room and unpacked for you while the maid runs a bath. If you are peckish irrespective of the time of day or night, special staff are on hand to indulge you. A smoked salmon omelette for you Sir and caviar and bliny for you Madame? No problem.

The Guarda Golf has all facilities expected of a five-star hotel including three restaurants, a spa, beauty treatments and spacious swimming pool. One can easily spend a day using the facilities and they are open to the public too. The plus is an underfloor heated balcony which prevents an icy surface from forming in winter.

Each of the 25 rooms in the hotel, has control system which is easily accessed for the entertainment programme or to operate the blinds. In addition there is a purifier and humidifier because the air is dry outside. The rooms are furnished with magnificent dark wood headboards as well as two huge side cabinets.

In the lounge, there is a playroom for children to keep them occupied while their parents can enjoy a drink or a snack. To tantalize the guests the hotel makes its own patisserie on the premises.

The person who handpicked everything is the owner, Nati Felli, who is Brazilian but now lives in Crans-Montana with her Swiss husband Giancarlo and daughter.

"I am not just selling a bed," said Nati. "I have a double responsibility as people are coming to my home and paying for the

Bella Lui hotel

10

privilege. To keep us on our toes we are members of hotel organizations who send round anonymous checkers and award points. We tend to get 80% and over."

The hotel lives up to its name and offers extras for golfers. There is an indoor and outdoor golf practice area, private golf cars, green fee reservations and transfers to the golf courses if required.

"We run a five star hotel," said Nati, "and nothing is too much to do. In the middle of winter, a guest announced that they would like to have a watermelon the next day. It arrived at their table for dinner."

Nati and Giancarlo met in 1994 at a joint alumni function for their respective schools in Bluche. He had graduated at the Les Roches high school which had later become Les Roches International School of Hotel Management. (See separate entry). She is graduate of Les Roches and her dream had always been to run a hotel.

Hotel Bella Lui
Route du Zotset 8
Montana
027 481 31 14
info@bellalui.ch
www.bellalui.ch

The 3-star historic hotel opened in 1930 and is today acknowledged as an exceptional example of modern architecture, retaining many features of its era. (See separate entry Architecture). The lounge with original furnishings or enjoying the sun on a period chaise longue or a relaxed meal with old fashioned silver tableware

will perhaps be highlights of your stay at 1500 m.

"The hotel is surrounded by a private forest," said Rahel Isenschmied, the manager, "and the hotel enjoys a sunny location, offering splendid views over the Alps and Lake Grenon."

It is located in the centre of the resort and the ski lifts are just a few minutes walk from the hotel.

Hotel Royal
Ehanoun 10
Crans
027 485 95 95
info@hotel-royal.ch
www.hotel-royal.ch

The hotel Royal, a Crans-Montana 5-star institution was completely renovated in 2012 and encompasses the idea of relaxed luxury with its spa and indoor swimming pool and special children's area.

The ambiance is one of light open spaces suited to mountain chic. The cosy atmosphere is induced by fireplace and the English bar and beige walls. Highlights in the reception include the two candelabras, one of deer antlers and the other a contemporary version with hanging bulbs that constantly change colours.

The bedrooms are part of the chalet style that cocoons the guests with wooden panels and elegant wooden furniture and indirect lighting. The majority of rooms are south-facing with balconies providing a combination of views from the distant peaks to residential trees and golf greens that turn into ski areas in winter. They are fitted with the latest technology including high speed WIFI, HD flat screens with over a 100 television channels, a media hub and iPod connections.

"Crans-Montana is a small living city," said Cyril Marcou, the Managing director who is French but studied hospitality in Glion. "It definitely has an international feel about it and you find people of all nations here."

Art de Vivre Hôtel Restaurant & Spa
Route de Fleurs des Champs 17
Montana
027 481 33 12
art-vivre@bluewin.ch
www.art-vivre.ch

It is a small family run 4-star hotel with 24 rooms but guests can enjoy facilities offered by the luxury of a five-star. They can indulge in a gourmand menu; take physio, osteo and beauty treatments; have massages; cavort in the swimming pool and jacuzzi; and take a steam bath, sauna and work out in fitness. The big bonus is the view. It is nothing short of spectacular.

The habits of guests have changed over the past decades. At one time, they would come to the resort and spend a minimum of a week. Some would even come on a month's holiday. But now the average is 2.6 days.

"The lives of the guests are in the fast track and stressed," said Joseph who runs the Art de Vivre with his wife, Séverine and is the third generation of hoteliers. "Before they come, they want to know

everything. Which slopes are open, whether we have WIFI, what the dinner menu is like and the weather forecast? When they arrive, I try to calm them down. I ask them, are you sure you want your iPad? Some confess later that they locked their iPad in the safe and thanked me."

It was a tough decision to stay in the hotel business. The Bonvins went against the grain because during the property boom most people were turning their hotels into apartments or selling them and moving elsewhere. But they could not think of any other place where they would like to raise children.

Crans Ambassador
Route du Petit Signal 3
Montana
027 485 48 48
info@cransambassador.ch
www.cransambassador.ch

The 5-star hotel is promoting a new concept of luxury sport resort. This includes a ski in/ski out location next to the Cry d'Er ski lifts and a sport boutique that offers ski rentals - even Lacroix skis, golf equipment, mountain bikes, and a range of well known prêt-à-porter clothing.

The setting of the hotel is nothing less than spectacular because wherever you are your eyes are drawn outside to the views of Alpine summits.

As is expected the facilities include three restaurants, Le Restaurant and La Terrasse. But a nice surprise is the carnozet which will introduce visitors to the local tradition. This is the wine tasting room found

10

at any winemaker. Here the wines are sampled with the typical accompaniment in the Valais of rye bread, cheese and dried meat. Fondue and raclette is also offered as well as a range of regional vintages.

The Panoramic Bar Lounge is the place for the cognoscenti to be and to be seen. It has 180 degree views of the resort.

The choice of rooms vary from a single, a forest room to deluxe, premium and the top suite. There is also a spacious spa and a high tech gym.

Best Mountain Resort hotels

The three hotels, a 5-star Pas de L'Ours, and two 4-stars, L'Etrier and Aida Castel are run by the Bestenheider family and being being promoted under the brand of the Best Mountain Resort (BMR). They are what every visitor would expect to find at 1,500 m. - wooden chalets like the Swiss Heidi's and surrounded by a forest and overlooking lakes.

But guests get more at one of the Bestenheider hotels.

The woodwork inside is superb as Armand Bestenheider who is a perfectionist has seen to every detail. Wood is his passion and he has used old and new wood and different varieties including larch, pine and birch.

He is lucky because his daughters appreciated his philosophy of living.

"We were never forced to follow in his footsteps," said Géraldine who now runs the 4-star Hotel de l'Etrier. "But hotel living was a lifestyle for us as we spent most of our time in them. We had our meals there, were familiar with the staff and worked there during the holidays. It is natural that we are all became involved in hospitality. Severine who likes decoration runs the 5-star Pas de l'Ours and Stephanie who is the organizer has taken over the 4-star Aïda Castel."

The three hotels are being mostly promoted by Géraldine who is in charge of marketing. "My father is not the easiest person to work for. He uses the best craftsmen and although he has idea of something he wants, it can change in the reality. So people have to be flexible. But the result always touches on perfection."

Hotel de L'Etrier

Rue du Pas de L'Ours 31
Crans
027 485 4400
hotel.etrier@bluewin.ch
www. hoteletrier.ch

The 4-star hotel is located close to the slopes and the town centre and has 59 rooms which are tastefully decorated in wood. It also has a spa, indoor and outdoor swimming pools.

There are three restaurants including one on the terrace next to the swimming pool which is only open in summer and the Le fer à Cheval which has a traditional Swiss cuisine and the main restaurant with French-Italian cuisine. The lounge with its comfortable leather sofas has a cozy ambiance where guests can enjoy cocktails.

Hostellerie Du Pas de L'Ours, Relais & Châteaux

41, Rue de l'Ours

Crans
027 485 93 33
pasdelours@relaischateaux.com
www.pasdelours.ch

The 5-star hotel is a temple to wood and stone. The suites and junior suites have open fireplaces, jacuzzis and views of the snow-covered mountain peaks and a spa. It has a charming ambiance and features an unusual painting. It is of Felix, Pas de l'Ours's former resident donkey. In a cosy atmosphere, top Michelin chef, Franck Reynard is on hand at the gourmet restaurant where guests can savour a selection of vegetables, milk-fed lamb, bass, sea bream, mullet, venison and other culinary treats. (See separate entry). There is also a bistrot.

Hotel Aida Castel
Rue du Béthania
Montana
027 485 41 11
info@aida-castel.ch
www.aida-castel.ch

The 4-star Hotel Aida-Castel, built in a rustic style offers a breathtaking view of the Valaisian Alps. It has 61 rooms of various categories and is just a few steps from the centre of Montana and minutes away the centre and ski lifts.

The Verdi restaurant offers a four-course dinner with a wide range of a la carte French and Italian dishes. Typical regional products can be tried in the traditional restaurant "Valais."

Guests can relax comfortably in the winter garden of the hotel which provides access to the heated outdoor pool and enjoy the view. There is a sauna, steam bath and fitness area where breakfast can be served breakfast throughout the year.

Le Crans Hotel and Spa
Chemin du Mont-Blanc 1
Crans
027 486 60 60
info@lecrans.com
www.lecrans.com

Jolly's 5-Star
A Belgium couple, Mr and Mrs Jolly fell in love with Crans-Montana and decided to build a hotel which would give the same comfort to the guests as their own luxury home. The brief was to have a wine bar, a cigar lounge, a spa with all accoutrements, a restaurant and the 15 rooms and suites had to be special. They had to be named after mountain ranges worldwide such as the Atlas, the Rocky Mountains, the Urals, Everest, the Dolomites and Kilimanjaro.

To develop the theme of mountains, the Jollys hired the theatrical interior designer Christophe Decarpentrie to decorate the bedrooms. His approach was to create spaces to dream with rare tapestries and precious objects. The Urals has a charming print of the Tsar and his family over the fireplace and the muted color of the bedspreads and wall paper match the Russian period. But the luxury does not stop at the furnishings, the bedrooms are equipped with all-in-one electronic control modules for the DVD player with 200 preloaded movies, the plasma screen televisions with a set even above the jacuzzi in the marble

10

bathroom and Nespresso coffee machines.

"Our service is unobtrusive and discrete," said Paola Masciulli, director of the 5-star hotel. "But we can provide guests with whatever they require whether it is shopping - we have two limousines at our disposal, babysitters, dog walkers or a helicopter to ski on a glacier in Verbier or to collect them from the airport. Sometimes, the hotel is taken over for a private event like an anniversary. What guests appreciate is that everything here is arranged for their own convenience. The ski slopes are 100 m away and hiking trails are on the doorstep."

The gourmet restaurant which is on the premises with a creative chef and has a chef's table in the kitchen where up to eight diners can eat, attended by the cooking staff. (See entry Pierre Crépaud).

The spa offers the usual stuff as well as facials, hands and feet treatments, epilations or colourations. Here Decarpentrie created a serene atmosphere with little touches like a small Indian temple crowned with candles and orchids, an old wooden bench from colonial times and a background of green with jade marble stone from Indonesia.

"The guest is always right when they stay with us," said Paola Masciulli. "All my team is trained to act quickly to any requests or comments of the guests. We like to excel in a flawless service."

Crans Luxury lodges
chemin de la Nationale 1-10
027 480 35 08

078 896 0479
info@cransluxurylodges.com
www.cransluxurylodges.com

Crans Luxury Lodges is a novel concept. You have the facilities of a boutique hotel in the privacy of your own luxury chalet. There is a private spa, an entertainment area, a dining room, kitchen and living room with a fireplace. Then if you wish you can have the whole package of around-the-clock concierge, a private chef, transportation, a full maid service and waking up to a mountain breakfast. But you also have the choice of simply taking the key and not being disturbed during your stay.

For companies, you can hold conferences from 10 up to 50 people. The environment is ideal for team building because it is secluded and on the doorstep for in and out skiing as well as hiking.

The man behind the innovative idea is Julien de Preux. The land on which he built the three buildings with the five chalets belonged to his ancestors for the past 400 years.

"Crans-Montana is a world class resort and I felt I had to come up with something that matched the aspirations of the cosmopolitan visitors," he said. "The chalet girls concept with the all-in package was outdated. So were staff who wore uniforms. Flexibility was the key to cater to a global market. Some wanted maid service once a week while others wanted clean linen every day."

Julien's background is hospitality which
he studied at Lausanne. He learnt how
to grow a business and to create opportunities. When he came to live in the
Crans-Montana, he realized that he had to
be open-minded and to keep his ears and
eyes open to everything coming his way.
But the key was to be proactive.

"We have found that satisfied customers
are our best ambassadors," he said. "One
couple celebrated their wedding anniversary with fireworks on the slopes and then
the husband surprised his wife by ordering
special diamond earrings. We had to bring
a jeweler over from Geneva."

Hotel Le Mont-Paisible
chemin du Mont-Paisible 12
Montana
027 480 21 61
info@montpaisible.ch
www.montpaisible.ch

The 3-star hotel is situated 1.5 km from the
centre of the resort and only 200 m from
the Violettes cableway station. It is in a
peaceful and rustic setting, facing the Alps
and dominating the Rhone Valley. It has a
sauna and all rooms have a balcony.

The hotel is known for their special golf
packages which include green fees in
Crans-Montana and Leuk. In the winter,
they have special packages including ski
lift passes which can be obtained at the
hotel.

10

Chapter 11. Art and Culture

Although, Crans-Montana never had a school of artists like Savièse, a village just above Sion, it attracted artists and writers like Katherine Mansfield and Elizabeth von Arnim who extolled the landscape and panoramic views. The first painter who depicted the resort was Albert Muret from Morges, lake Geneva. He bought a chalet in Lens in 1902 and painted scenes of the landscape and people from the village.

But it was the great Swiss painter, Ferdinand Hodler who did justice to the high plateau. In 1915, Hodler spent the summer in Crans-Montana where his son Hector was being treated for TB. He was inspired by the incredible panoramic views of the mountain range from Mont Blanc to the Matterhorn. Later, he would immortalize the view of lake Geneva and the Mont Blanc which he painted from his apartment and studio in Geneva.

The life of Ferdinand Hodler, one of the great Swiss painters was always dogged by death and in the end, he used the experience to develop his talent. By the age of eight, his father and two younger brothers died of TB. His mother who had remarried also succumbed to the disease by the time he was 14 as did subsequently all of his remaining siblings.

"In the family there was an atmosphere of all-embracing death," he recalled later. "Eventually, it seemed to me that there was always a dead person in the house, as if it had to be this way."

Later, in 1908, he met the love of his life, Valentine Godé-Darel, a Parisienne who was 20 years younger and had moved to Geneva where she sang in operettas and painted porcelain for a living. After she gave birth to their daughter Paulette, she became ill with what was first thought of as being TB but later turned out to be cancer.

He recorded the progress of her illness and suffering in over 18 paintings, a series, which was unique in the history of art and it represented her death. It could only be compared with Holbein's unsparing naturalistic depiction of a decomposing corpse and represented her death with scientific accuracy. Her open mouth, sunken eyes, her claw-like hands followed the recognizable medical pattern of death.

She died on January 25, 1915 in her home in Vevey at the age of 40.

11

"When you accept death," he said, "when you let it become part of your consciousness and will, that's when you really create great art!...Just being aware of that gives the thought of death gigantic force."

He spent a holiday during the summer, August and September of that year in Crans-Montana with his wife Berthe and Paulette, his daughter from his model Valentine Godé-Darel. He drew and painted some 20 landscapes which included the Weisshorn, Bietschhorn, Bella Tolla, Becs de Boson and Vallon de Réchy, Zinalrothorn and several of the lake Etang Long. "Colour is more prominent in these paintings," said Paul Müller of the Swiss Institute of Art Research (SIK-ISEA). "He had been labeled a drawer rather a colourist by critics and he changed his style in the paintings from Montana."

Hodler believed that landscape painting 'should show us nature made greater and simpler, pared of insignificant details.... If I want to express the infinity of a horizontal line of mountains or a lake, I always have to ask myself where it has to start and where I have to cut it off.'

Hodler was a painter who crossed borders. His nudity in the *Die Nacht* or *The Night* caused a scandal, as did his powerful Expressionist paintings of the dying and the dead mistress Valentine Gode-Darel and his series of rhythmic figures.

His experience with death also gave him a lust for life. He married twice and had numerous affairs. His first wife was Bertha Stucki whom he met in Interlaken and whom he portrayed in the risqué painting of *Das Strumpfband* or *The garter* - she displayed her leg up to the knee. They divorced after a brief and tempestuous union in 1891.

His second wife, Berthe Jacques, was a schoolteacher who lived in Geneva where he had his studio. They married in 1898 and she modeled for him in several paintings including *Der Tag* or the *Day*. It was one of the works for which he won international praise and the gold medal of honour.

The couple moved into a luxurious apartment at 29 Quai du Mont Blanc in Geneva which was furnished by Josef Hoffmann who was a founding member of the Secession and a friend of Klimt. Towards the end of his life he returned to landscape painting and his favorite subjects were Swiss mountains, lakes, glaciers trees and rocks.

During the last few months of his life, when he rarely left the apartment for health reasons, he had embarked on a series of views of lake Geneva with Mont Blanc at different times of the day. He died in May 19, 1918 in Geneva at the age of 65. Paulette was adopted by Hodler's wife, Berthe.

"Hodler is underrated as a painter," said Ulf Kuester who is a curator of the Beyeler Foundation, Basel. "He died too early and was isolated in Switzerland. He was part of modern art and innovative. If you look at his paintings of lake Geneva with Mont Blanc (1916 and 1917) you will see that he

was one step away from Mark Rothko."

Art Centre: Pierre Arnaud Fondation

Mr Culture

Daniel Salzmann who established the Foundation Pierre Arnaud is an influential figure in the art world. At a stroke, he has changed the nature of Crans-Montana for it will become a centre of art and attract international audiences. The last time such a major event occurred in the Valais was the opening of the Fondation Pierre Gianadda almost 40 years ago by Leonard Gianadda and it has had some 9 million visitors.

"Crans-Montana is a ski station that can't exist on seasons which only last for several weeks," he said. "Culture has an important role to play too. In the past, it appealed to artists from Ferdinand Hodler who painted magnificent landscapes of the surroundings, Charles Muret and René Auberjonois to Katherine Mansfield and Charles-Ferdinand Ramuz. And Stravinsky spent an afternoon here."

The Pierre Arnaud which opens in December 2013 will be innovative in terms of the two exhibitions it will mount every year.

"It has two unique objectives," he said. "The first is to compare and contrast Swiss painting with major international movements that began in Europe in the 19th and 20th centuries. The second is is to bring together Western and non-Western art."

Talented choreographer
Salzmann is also a talented choreographer

11

who has scripted dance performances depicting lives of Mozart and Egon Schiele. He wrote the script and directed the ballet *Mozart, a Life, a Requiem* in 2002 in which the famous ballerina Lucia Laccara played the composer. She has won several awards and was the principal dancer for Roland Petit who created four ballets for her. For Mozart, Salzmann collaborated with the composer and pianist Richard Rentsch and choreographer,Gérard Bohbot.

In 2011, Salzmann who was fascinated by the painter Egon Schiele, wrote a script and choreographed the ballet *I, Eternal Child*, for which Richard Rentsch and Orazio Sciortino wrote the music. Stephane Victoria formerly of the Bejart Ballet in Lausanne danced the role of Egon Schiele against a background of his paintings.

Salzmann has a vision of what he wants for his projects and finds the right talented people to implement them. It is a win-win situation. He has a phenomenal energy and stamina to see them through even if it takes 20 years to execute them. The Foundation Pierre Arnaud under his guidance will be a resounding success.

The Building

The building itself resembles a landscape painting because its mirrored surface reflects the panoramic view of the lake in front and the mountains. It generates energy through solar panels that ensure an optimal thermal insulation for the works of art and enough light for exhibitions inside.

"It was important for the foundation to have an elegant and modern art centre," he said, "that meets the highest standards in terms of energy efficiency. It's a low energy consumption building."

Besides being a distinguished patron of the arts, Salzmann has entrepreneurial abilities which were demonstrated as a teenager when he organised an exhibition of friends' paintings.

The Foundation which covers an area of 1,000 square metres in Lens is devoted to the memory of the French art collector, Pierre Arnaud who settled in the Valais. The building will house his art collection which began with paintings from the Savièse School.

His daughter Sylvie Salzmann is the unofficial ambassador for the foundation. The building which is designed by the architects JP Emery and partners has gallery space on two levels. (See separate entry). The ground floor has a restaurant and terrace with views of the mountains.

Curator

Christophe Flubacher is a curator extraordinaire. He studied religion and philosophy before he turned the corner and became an art historian and art critic. His background enables him to come up with unusual angles to art.

"When we look at a picture," he said, "we tend to make a quick decision whether we like it or not. But this wrong because it's like opening a book, there is so much to read in it." He gives the example of Ferdinand Hodler's painting of *La Rade de Geneva et Mt Blanc* (1914). It is a mixture of landscape as well as symbolism. In the background are the mountains and in the foreground the lake and six swans. It can be easily dismissed unless you recognize that the swans are in a geometric order and face left to right. There is always present the harmony of nature.

As an art critic, he tended to give good reviews of an artist's work. Then one day the editor suggested that he should also give bad reviews. He understood later when a concentration camp survivor spoke of her experiences. At one point she said, "It gave me hope." The interviewer was puzzled by her answer because of the Nazi's brutality and evil. "There was a little good in the friendship and solidarity of the inmates," she replied.

In art it is essential to understand the past. Flubacher cites the stain glass window in Chartres cathedral - lancets below the south rose window, which depict the four prophets as giants and the evangelists as life-sized figures perched on their shoulders.

"We are as dwarfs mounted on the shoulders of giants," said Bernard of Chartres, "so that we can see more and further than they; yet not by virtue of the keenness of our eyesight, nor through the tallness of our stature, but because we are raised and borne aloft upon that giant mass." He was comparing the modern scholar of the 12th century to the ancient scholars of Greece and Rome.

"My aim for the Foundation Pierre Arnaud is education and freedom," said Flubacher.

"In the exhibits, we explain what we are showing and our displays enable visitors to have a freedom of walking where they want. The displays are not arranged in any order chronological or otherwise. It is if you like, the paintings are in conversations with each other."

Tips: Visit the museums in Sion, in Savièse which display the Savièse school and the Pierre Gianadda, Martigny, which mounts international exhibitions.

Classics, rock and pop
Somnets du Classique

Classical music has always been part of the cultural life of Crans-Montana. Christine Rey established Somnets du ClassiquE over a decade ago and her festival is dedicated to the virtuosi of the future. The aim is to nurture, support and guide young talented musicians. One of the means is to provide scholarships and to date some CHF 140,000 has been awarded.

"The study of classical music requires determination and work," she said, "the artists know better than anyone. To give us concert quality, it takes hours of effort from these musicians. The mountains need to be climbed in order to reach the summits. It's important to encourage the young."

On one occasion, Christine Rey had a 13 year old Zhao Mélodie, a Sino-Swiss pianist who was accompanied by the Russian Symphony orchestra. Since then Mélodie wrote her own composition for solo piano and in 2011, she was awarded the Leenaards scholarship. Subsequently, she recorded Liszt's 12 Transcendental Studies

11

Maestro Shlomo Mintz

and then played these complete cycles at the Victoria Hall, Geneva.

For details of the summer and winter programme see the website: www.som-nets-du-classique.ch and for tickets contact 0789197210 or 027 4833278

Crans-Montana Classics

The other musical organisation is Crans-Montana Classics. Jean Bonvin who headed the International Music Festival in Sion for a decade is the president. Maestro Shlomo Mintz is the Artistic director. Crans-Montana Classics was launched at a prestigious concert in January 1, 2013 with the Cameristi della Scala and Maestro Mintz as the soloist.

A key element in the programme is the Master Classes. These offer unique opportunities for talented young violinists to benefit from the teaching of the most renowned professors in the world. Among them are Zakhar Bron, Victor Danchenko, Cihat Askin as well as Maestro Mintz. The aim is to identify young talented violinists and to enrich their experience through practice. The participants will also be given encouragement and support in the future steps in their careers.

Maestro Shlomo Mintz who was born in Moscow is an Israeli violinist, violist and conductor. His family immigrated to Israel when he was two. He studied with Ilona Feher who introduced him to Isaac Stern and whom later became his mentor. He began his career as a soloist at the age of 11 with the Israeli Philharmonic under Zubin Mehta. Soon after when Itzhak Perlman fell ill, he was asked by Mehta to play Paganini's First Violin Concerto.

In 2012, he celebrated his 50th anniversary on the concert stage and launched the Online Music Academy. It offers the opportunity to obtain the mastery and musical sensitivity to interpret the great classical repertoire.

Jean Bonvin has ambitious plans for Crans-Montana Classics and already has introduced a series of original Concerts Off in the pastures of Colombire and at the Hotel Royal. (See separate entry). "Music has been the language of life par excellence throughout the ages unfettered by time and space," he said."We are committed to a series of remarkable and unusual musical encounters, connecting classical and world music and bringing together experienced artists and young talents for a unique musical event."

For details of the summer and winter programmes see the website www:cmclassics. ch and for tickets contact 079 469 5743.

Caprices

The rock and pop festival Caprices is in its 10th year and the programme is ambitious as ever. The headliners this year included included Björk, Fatboy Slim, M, Mika, Alice Cooper and Roger Hodgson. The event was extended to nine days from four the year before and is now one of the top five biggest festivals in Switzerland with a budget of some CHF 9 million. Daniel Salzmann, the notable patron of the arts, was approached at the outset and agreed to be the president of the Caprices Festival Foundation. (See separate entry).

"It's a great venture," he said. "Perhaps, a bit crazy, well even absolutely crazy." But with him onboard, it was bound to be successful. Some 60,000 people attended in 2013 and besides rock and pop there was hip-hop, soul, R & B, folk and electronica. For details see the website www:caprices-festival.ch

11

Chapter 12. Communes

Crans-Montana as an entity does not exist. People know that the village Crans is on the west side and Montana is on the east. But the land is owned and is dissected by six communes. From the west to the east along the Bernese alps are Icogne, Lens, Chermignon, Montana, Randogne and Mollens. The reason is that each commune needed to have a strip of land rising from the Rhone valley to the Alpine meadows to accommodate their migrations every year. In the spring and autumn, they worked in the vineyards, in the summer they transported the cattle to graze in the alpage while they stayed put in the winter. At one time, many families had herds up there but nowadays it has dwindled drastically. One person who still continues the tradition is Doris Mudry from Lens who makes cheese on the alpage de Mondralèche. However, in keeping with modernity she trucks the herd up and uses milking equipment. You can visit her up there and buy her cheese. (See separate entry)

Icogne

Icogne boasts two attractions. The Zeuzier dam which located in the alpage and a building designed by the architect Jean-Marie Ellenberger - the church of La Croix de Mission.

Marlène van der Vliet was born into one of the prominent families of Icogne, the Praplan. The name derives from the patois, which means flat grazing.

"I was born in the village which had a population of some 300 people," she said, "and everybody knew everybody and had an eye out for everybody. When I was a child we spent most of the time outdoors and only came inside to eat and sleep. At school there were only two classes, one for children from 6-9 years and the other for children from 10-13 years. It was like you see in Albert Anker paintings."

One of her happiest memories was when she was a three-year old. She would accompany her mother to Lens in winter whenever there was a funeral. It was boring for her to sit through the mass but she always looked forward to sledding down with her mother.

Once a year, there was a memorable scene at school when they were visited by a woman who came to teach them about dental hygiene. They would all have to line up in front of the small fountain in the town square as they did not have running water at school. Each of the pupils were

12

Marlène van der Vliet

children and sometimes we would just invite them to eat with us. Other times, we would hand over old clothes which we no longer needed."

Marlène was a bit of a rebel and studied Reiki because she felt it followed in the culture of the Celts who had lived in the Valais around 200 BC. They had sacred places with supernatural forces. Practitioners of Reiki believe that they are transferring universal energy through their palms which promotes healing and a state of equilibrium.

"It was so foreign to my parents," she said," that my father once came to see me and I gave him a Reiki treatment. 'Now I see what you do,' he said and left afterwards.'"

For Marlène, it was difficult to be a free-thinker in a patriarchal society. She is a woman of courage like Gabrielle Nanchen, also from Icogne who was elected to the national council in 1971 when suffrage for Swiss women was introduced. Marlène was 19 at the time when she met Eddy van der Vliet, a 35 year old Dutchman whom she subsequently married. (See separate entry). He was in real estate and was flying from one city to the other.

given toothpaste to put on their toothbrush. Duly they began brushing their teeth when suddenly cows appeared to drink from the fountain. There was nothing they could do except wait with the awful toothpaste in their mouths until the cows were finished to rinse it out with water.

"There were some people who were poor," she said. "For example, families with 10

"I was happy in Crans-Montana where I had strong roots," she said, "and I had no desire to leave, let alone to travel. He respected my wishes and settled in the resort. We held our wedding at a Dutch friend's hotel. When we had an apero at a table near the fireplace, I said to Eddy, 'My best wish is that we can live here.'

Bisse

Bell ringer

Four years later, the Dutch friend sold the place and it became our home.'"

Lens

The village which was once the capital village of Grand Lens community has several attractions. The statue of Christ the King - 35 metres tall, built in 1935 and cost CHF 35,000; St Peter's church which has one of the largest carillons in Switzerland - 24 bells; and the two ancient bisses - the Sillonin from the 14th century and the Grand Bisse from the 15th century. Last but not least, is Monument restaurant which is recommended.

Gérard Bonvin like most of the inhabitants in Crans-Montana is proud of his roots. However, he has gone the extra mile to find out more and commissioned the

12

local genealogist, Jean-Pierre Duc to do research into his ancestors who go back as far as 1399 when they came from France and Italy.

He was chuffed to find more information about his great grandfather, Joseph Bonvin, who had 11 children. He was born in the little village Chelin before moving to Lens. Like many mountain farmers his life consisted of looking after cattle, growing crops and tending to the the vineyards of Lens.

But his enthusiasm for hunting brought him into contact with the painter Albert Muret and the writer Charles-Ferdinand Ramuz who both later became friends. He would go chamois hunting with Muret who mentioned him in the foreword of his book, *Nemrod & Cie,* and painted a picture of him. Ramuz also wrote about him in his book *Le Règne de l'esprit malin.*

One of the strange things Gérard Bonvin found was that a relative whose wife died married another woman with the same name. His daughter who was three at the time never guessed that her 'mother' was really her stepmother until she found out the truth at 18.

Gérard Bonvin who gained a degree in economics in Geneva is a cousin of Christian Barras as his aunt Odette married Gaston Barras, Mr Golf. He works in the same real estate agency as his cousin.

12

Chermignon

It is known for the St George's fete in April when the commune offers rye bread to all the inhabitants. The cafe restaurant Chermignon which has a B & B is recommended. (See separate entry.)

Alexandre Borgeat who was born in Chermignon is a banker. He is passionate about politics and is the president of one of the political parties in the village. Today there is a movement for fusion of all the communes. The process began with a survey organized by Association of the Six Communes of Crans-Montana which was positive on the issue. However, Lens which is the largest village in the commune voted to reject the issue.

"This is the strangeness of our system," said Borgeat. "However, I am sure that we will come round to fusion. That's what I enjoy about politics."

Maître Serge Sierro is a prominent lawyer and politician who lives in Sierre. He has a soft spot for Crans-Montana because his wife was born there. "It is indispensable to develop cultural activities in the resort," he said, "because it is a suitable environment for living the whole year. It has easy access, a dry and sunny climate and diversity of activities and good shopping."

He graduated in law at the University of Geneva in 1973. He followed with a notary degree in 1975 and became an advocate for the canton of Valais in 1982. He entered local politics early and was first on the council of the commune of Sierre before being elected President (1988-1992). He then became a member of the Cantonal government in the Valais (1988-1992) where he was President twice. He served as Head of Education, Social Affairs and Culture and Sport.

He is also a member of several boards including the Château de Villa foundation in Sierre and is President of the Advisory Board of Julius Bär for the Valais. He practices law in Sion where he is a specialist in advising wealthy foreigners who want to settle in the canton on the forfeit or lump sum tax. The Valais offers advantageous conditions compared to other cantons.

He is involved in several cultural associations in canton Valais: Fondation du conservatoire de Sion (Classical Music), Fondation Interface (Music, Dance and Visual Arts), Institut de recherche ophtalmologique (Institute of ophthalmology research) and Mediplan (an Institute of research on aromatic and medicinal plants).

Montana

In the 19th century two important events occurred here. The first hotel was built in 1893, hotel du Parc and it was discovered that dry Alpine air and sunny climate was good for the treatment of tuberculosis. This led to the building of TB clinics. Claude-Gérard Lamon who is the president of the Montana Commune is a banker. He was born in the house near the Montana Catholic church and is proud that it still exists.

His grandparents undertook several migrations a year. "It involved the trek of the

Montana

whole family and animals," he said. "In the case of my grandmother there was a mule, a pig, two goats, six chickens and a cat which was carried in a bag. The family spent the winter in Diogne in a house with two rooms - a kitchen and a bedroom. In March they would go down to Corin to prune the grapevines and return again in September to pick grapes. In summer they would be in Montana with the gardens and to graze cows on the alpage."

Randogne

The British novelist, Elizabeth von Arnim, built a chalet in Bluche, at the beginning of the 20th century. She was a widow and lived there with her concierge, his wife, the jeunne fille and her Swiss dog, Coco. Isabelle Bagnoud-Loretan who was born

12

in Geneva, lives with her husband in Randogne, the main village of the commune. She is a journalist and Editor-in-Chief of La vie à Crans-Montana which is a lifestyle magazine published bi-annually. She also writes for Le Journal de Sierre and Le Nouvelliste. But does it seem feasible that someone who was brought up in a city with a political science degree could bury herself in a resort of little villages?

"Crans-Montana is an exceptional place," she said. "It attracts a cosmopolitan crowd who are impressed that the people who were born here, still live here. The resort is not like all the other touristy places which look the same and people from cities come to live for a few weeks in little wooden chalets like Heidi. When my friends from Geneva visit, they are surprised by our lifestyle. They meet interesting people at parties, they're impressed with how many people I know and that people smile here. Unlike Geneva where it's hard to live and most people go around with unfriendly expressions."

Isabelle was struck by the landscape and nature when she first came. She enjoys skiing and ski touring. What she delights in is being in the mountains with her husband. "Sometimes you're up on the glacier totally alone with the sunset," she said. "What a joy!"

Mollens

A unique feature of the commune is the hamlet of Colombire (2000 m) which has a small cheese-making museum and several small chalets called mayens. The chalets replicate the ones used by the herders of animals which grazed on the alpage in the summer.

The hamlet provides an insight into 'vertical living' in mountain villages. Seasonal migration or remuage was necessary to meet the needs of keeping cattle and growing crops.

Each year villagers moved from one residence to another for a limited period. It was a caravan of family members, the priest, the schoolteacher and their livestock - cattle, goats and sheep and pets. During the winter, families lived in their main residence and kept their livestock with them. In the spring and autumn they moved down to the valley to work in the vineyards. Then in the summer after the snow had melted, they moved up with their livestock to the high mountain pasture or alpage. There they would stay in a little chalet or mayens to take care of the livestock. A cheese-making mayens was also built so that the milk could processed on site instead of being transported down to the valley. As the cows grazed on lush meadows, the Alpine cheese had a special flavor.

"The Colombire hamlet is based the idea of preserving the traditional heritage of the Valaisians," said Sandrine Espejo of the Colombire Hamlet Association, "which disappeared almost completely in the 1940s when the canton was industrialized. We reconstructed and relocated old mayens called Barzettes and Moubra which comprise the Eco-museum. A third one provides accommodation for two people."

Colombire hamlet

Barzettes has exhibits on the theme of movement and transport, past and present. Moubra gives an eyewitness account of what life was like then and the exhibits include the work on the alpage, memories of that time and atmosphere inside the dwelling and outside. Films compliment the exhibits. Later in the summer, there was haymaking and the hay was stored in the stable below the mayens while the people lived upstairs in two rooms. There was a kitchen and a bedroom where all the family slept.

The Colombire hamlet is in beautiful spot. It lies on the ski slopes of Crans-Montana and Aminona in winter and on the popular Tsittoret irrigation canal or bisse walking route in the summer. The hamlet consists of two clusters of buildings. In the lower part are the three mayens and in the upper part, the highlight is the striking restaurant and lookout which is a modern version of a mayens. It was designed by the Swiss architects Frundgallina and is characterized by a small pavilion-like structure

made of reinforced concrete on two levels. It has a terrace and the dining room with a single long table. The view of the mountains from the floor to ceiling window is fabulous.

"A number of outdoor activities are offered," said Sandrine. "Hikes along the bisses, flora and fauna tours, snowshoe walks by midnight as well as custom-made tours. During the summer, we make cheese to the delight of the children as they can join in. There is also an interesting cheese museum near the restaurant."

The eco-museum at Colombire hamlet is open at weekends from June-September and from July 15 - August 31 for 7 days a week. The restaurant is open every day from June 1 - end of August from 10 am until 6 pm. In September - middle October, it is open from 10 am until 5 pm. Closed on Mondays 079 220 3594.

Chapter 13. Funicular Railway

One of the convenient things about Crans-Montana is that it is easy to reach by funicular from the Rhone valley. But if you are weighed down by several pieces of luggage, you might find it easier to take a taxi from Sierre station. The funicular whisks you up to 1,500 m in 12 minutes from Sierre and is only 10 minutes walk from the station. If you need to go Chermingnon, Lens, Montana village, Crans or even Aminona, then you can catch a bus direct from the station.

The company SMC which had the foresight to build the funicular over a century ago, also offers a regular bus service every day of the year. A timetable is available from their website www.cie-smc.ch and there is a car park under the departure station in Sierre.

The funicular which is the longest in Europe is easy to operate, economical and ecological because the ascending and descending vehicles counterbalance each other. The energy to lift the vehicle going up is minimized by the one going down.

"The reason why some resorts had slow starts," said Patrick Cretton who runs SMC, "is the lack of mobility. Crans-Montana is lucky because we had mobility right from the start. Before the funicular it took several hours by mule to ascend to the resort."

Guillaume Rey is the second generation to operate the funicular. When he was a child he accompanied his father in the cab and dreamt of becoming a driver too. "The job is unlike any other," he said. "Each trip is different. The people, the landscape and the weather changes. Sometimes we come across stags, hinds and lots of foxes."

He keeps his eyes focused on the rails with one hand ready for a emergency. The fact that the rail is straight does not mean he can daydream. Sometimes he finds walkers or animals on the track.

13

Chapter 14. Wellness

Studio 21
Personal Training & Pilates Institute
Rue Louis Antille 2
Montana
+4127 480 33 00
studio21@bluewin.ch
www.studio21pilates.com

Personal trainers were once the personal preserve of celebrities and Hollywood actors. But times have changed and Crans-Montana also has its own trainer. She is Carine Bestenheider who has done wonders for both locals and foreign residents alike. The reason for her popularity is that she combines personal training with Pilates method which improves physical strength, flexibility and posture.
"Age or a person's physical condition doesn't matter when people come to me," she said, "I help them transform their body totally. They'll feel more energetic, more mobile and more relaxed from their very first session. They're surprised when they notice that their body responds with a more comfortable posture, easier movement and a new feeling of energy."
Carine is highly qualified. She began at the department of sports, fitness and aerobics, University of Lausanne and then went on to gain two postgraduate certificates in personal fitness training and became a Pilates master trainer in London. People come to her with the request that 'they just want to feel better.'

"One woman client was dissatisfied with her shape," she said. "I did all the assessments, took photos of her posture, measured muscle length and how she performed exercise. After several months of consistent training, people she knew didn't recognize her. Some thought she had had surgery and were confused by her new look. But the new shape she had acquired also caused the pain from a medical condition to disappear."

She can be found at Studio 21 where she offers a variety of exercises customized to training levels and abilities. These include sports nutrition and lifestyle coaching, golf conditioning, cardio training indoors and outdoors, functional strength, stretching with mobility and flexibility, spirals which is a new mind-body movement and Pilates. The programme is available to anyone from 10 to 80. Obviously, assessments are done according to their physical status.

Laguna Crans S.A.

Rue Centrale 7
Crans
027 481 30 00

The beauty and wellness salon which is located in an apartment block above the library has a calm ambiance and everything is impeccable. It has an international clientele and the level of professionalism is similar to establishments in New York, London or Paris. The treatments offered include face, body, massage, manicure and pedicure as well as exfoliation.

Right from the start Marianne Borgeaud who has run the salon for over 25 years offered natural plant based products like the Valmont collagen mask and the Carita renovator, the best exfoliating product available. Sisley for beauty care was added later. Loyalty has been a prime factor at the salon as some of the clients have remained with her from the beginning.

 Whereas in the past, it was important for the face to be sophisticated and lots of make-up was used, nowadays, the accent is on naturalness in face and body. Marianne who looks ten years younger than her real age is the best advertisement for the salon.

"I advise women of today who have to cope with increased stress," she said, "to use a product like Valmont DNA every day and visit a salon at least once a month."

Swiss Health Center

Allée Eysée Bonvin 7
Crans
027 481 3132
www.swisshealthcenter.ch
swisscenter.ch@bluewin.ch

The Swiss Health Center is conveniently situated in the Grand Hotel Golf & Palace. The location enables patients to make use of the luxury facilities such as the swimming pool and fitness room.

The centre offers a wide range of medical services and wellness treatments.

On the medical side, there is a full medical check-up programme from ECG, blood analysis to a sleep laboratory.

On wellness, there are treatments of herbal medicine and dietetic therapy, rejuvenation and aesthetic medicine. In addition, there is osteopathy and physiotherapy for skiing injuries and golfer's back problems.

"The centre offers a treatment plan to answer all a patient's personal needs and requests," said Dr C. Schroeder who in charge of the Swiss Health Center, "with high quality medical services. Our rejuvenating treatments are inspired by and based on the well known Maurice Mességué's methods."

14